Visions for Becoming

A book of photography and quotations
to inspire your authentic self

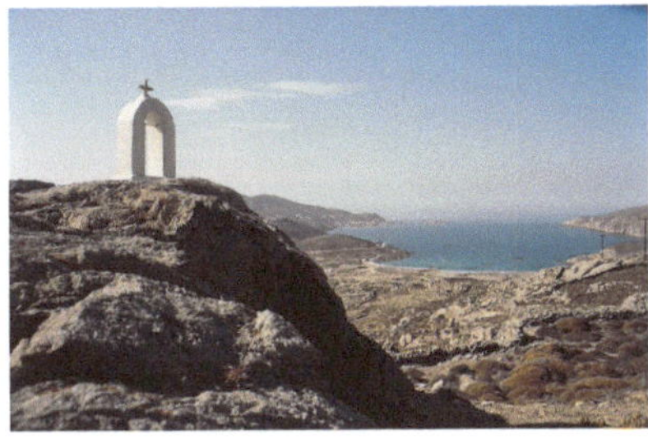

 Visit www.viewfromthepier.com

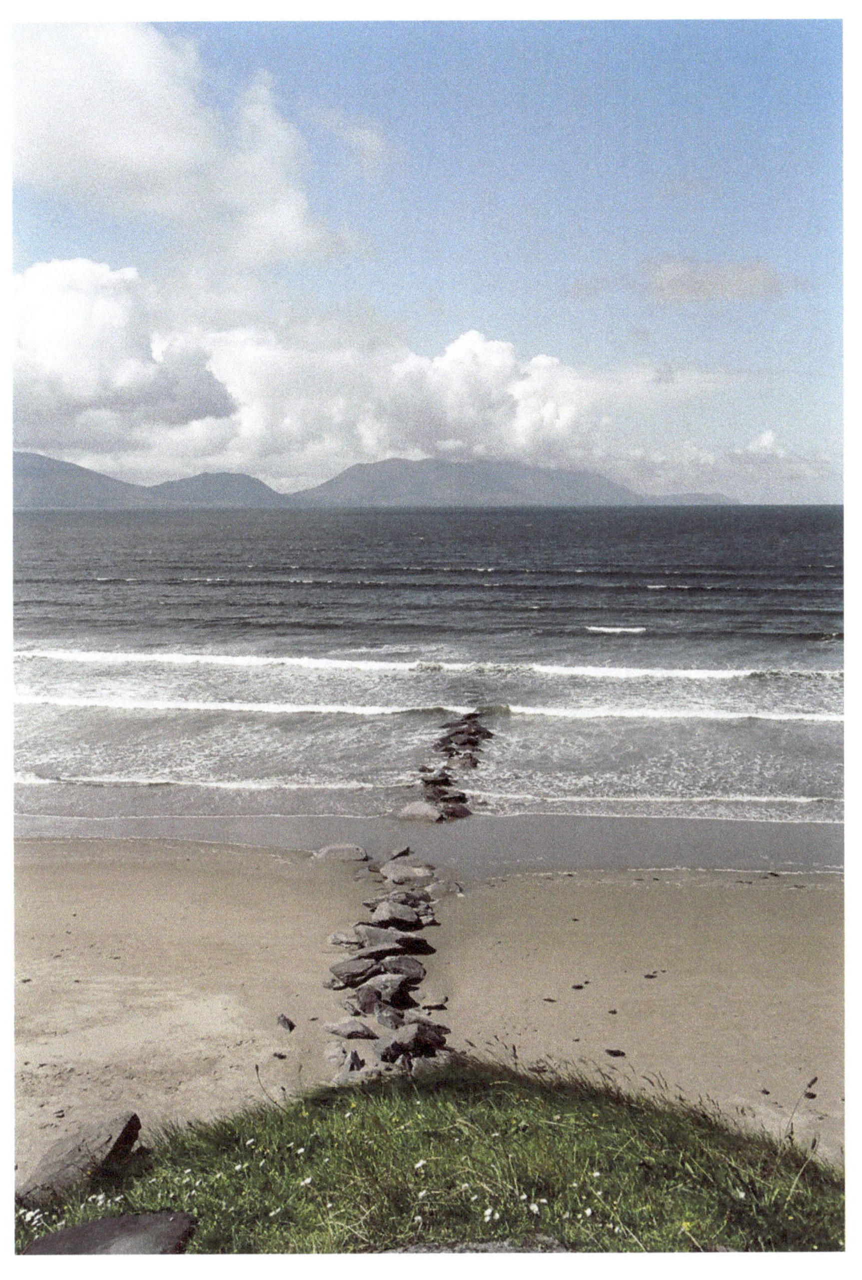

Inch Strand, Ireland

Follow your bliss.

--Joseph Campbell, 1904-1987

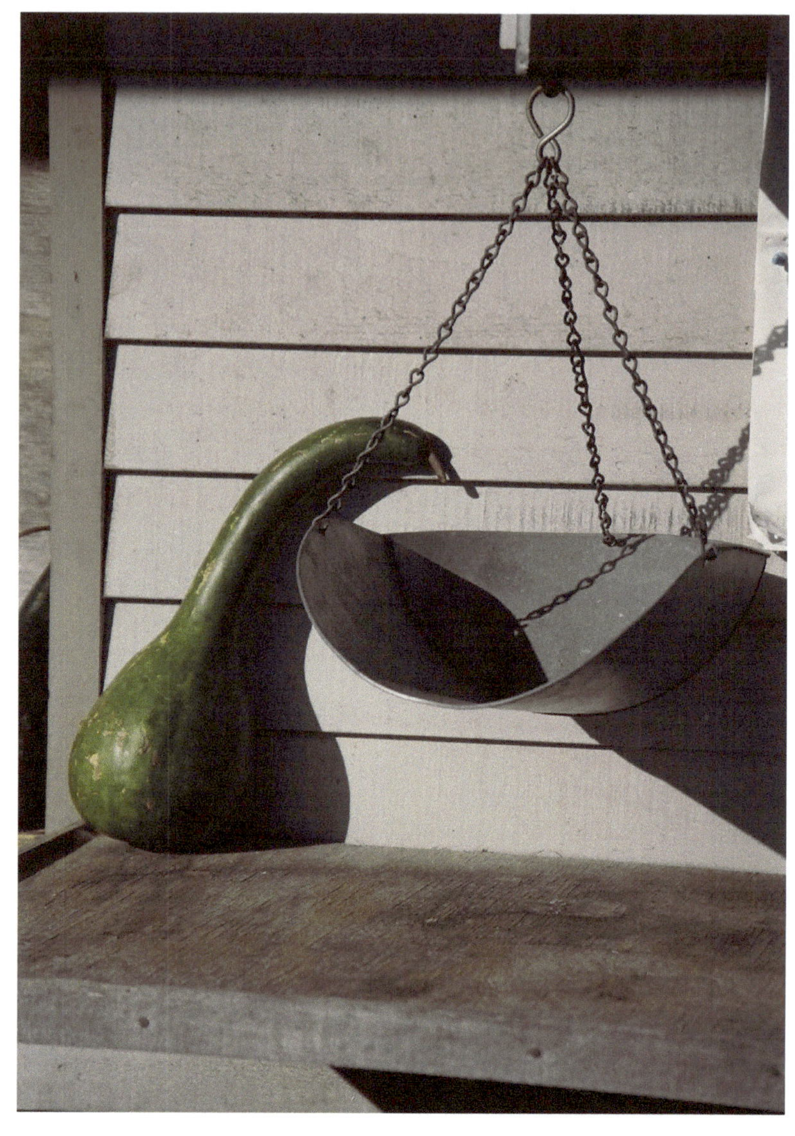

Southern Vermont

The highest courage is to dare to appear to be what one is.

--John Lancaster Spalding, 1840-1916

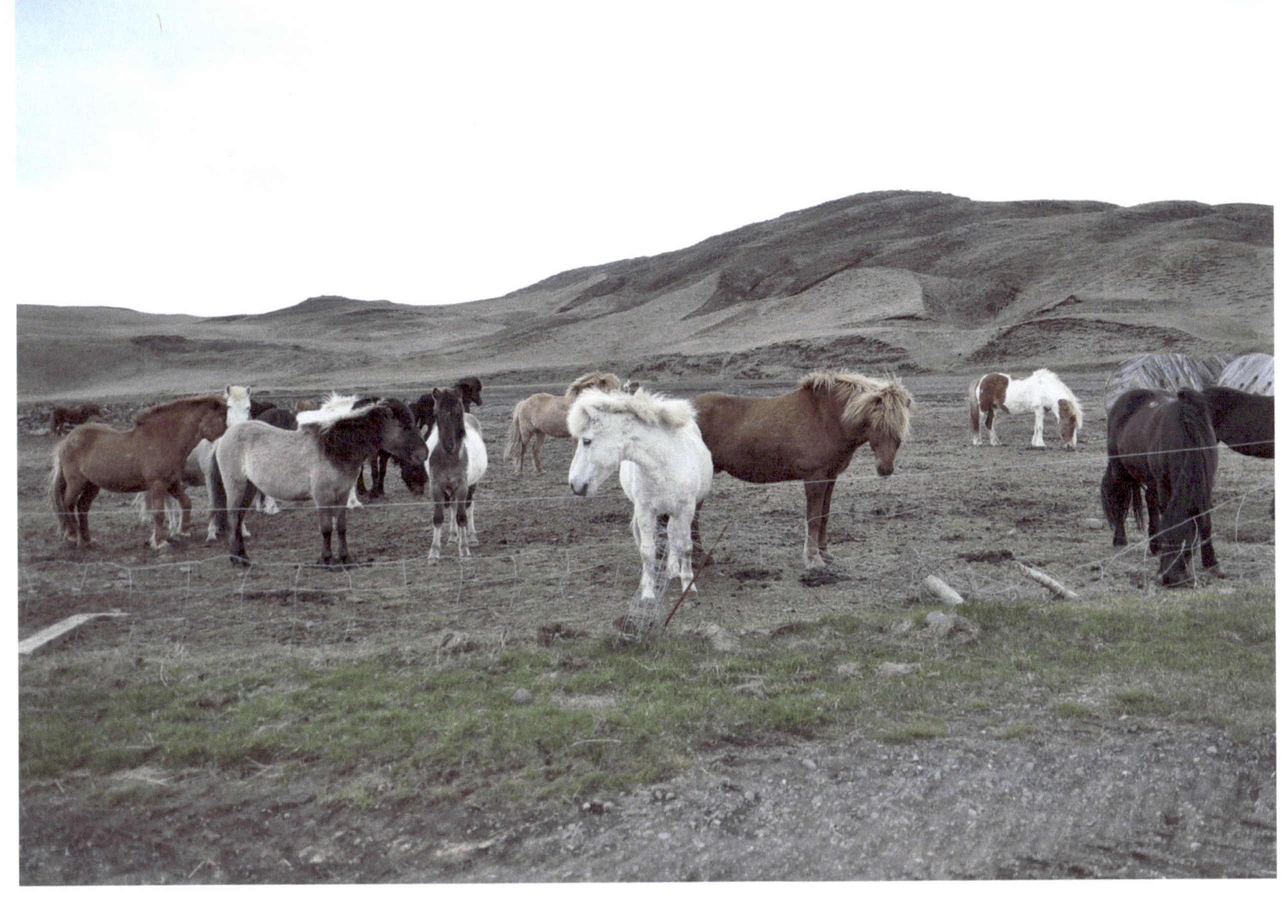

Iceland

If I am not for myself, who will be for me?
And if I am only for myself, what am I?
And if not now, when?
--Hillel, 30 B.C.-9 A.D.

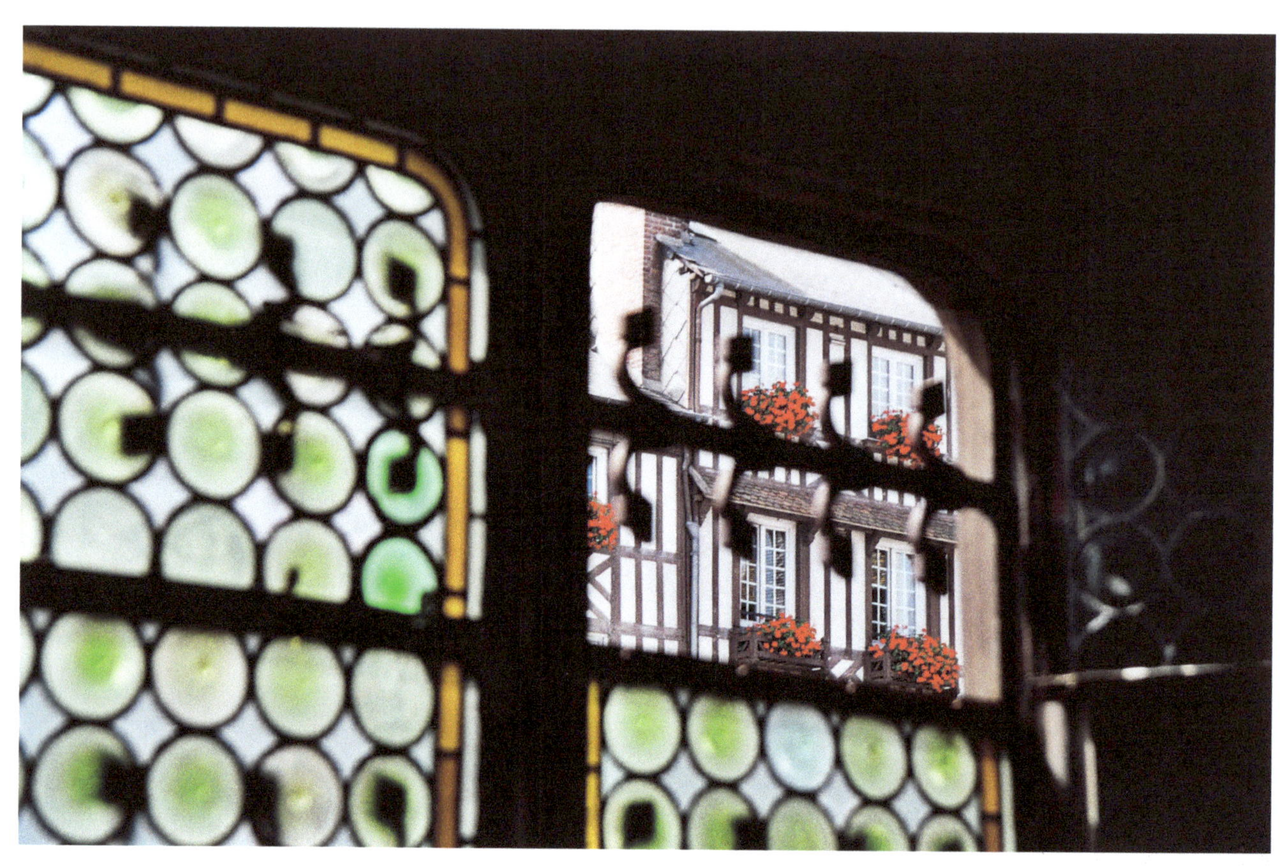

Honfleur, France

I was raised to sense what someone wanted me to be and be that kind of person.
It took me a long time not to judge myself through someone else's eyes.
--Sally Field, 1946-

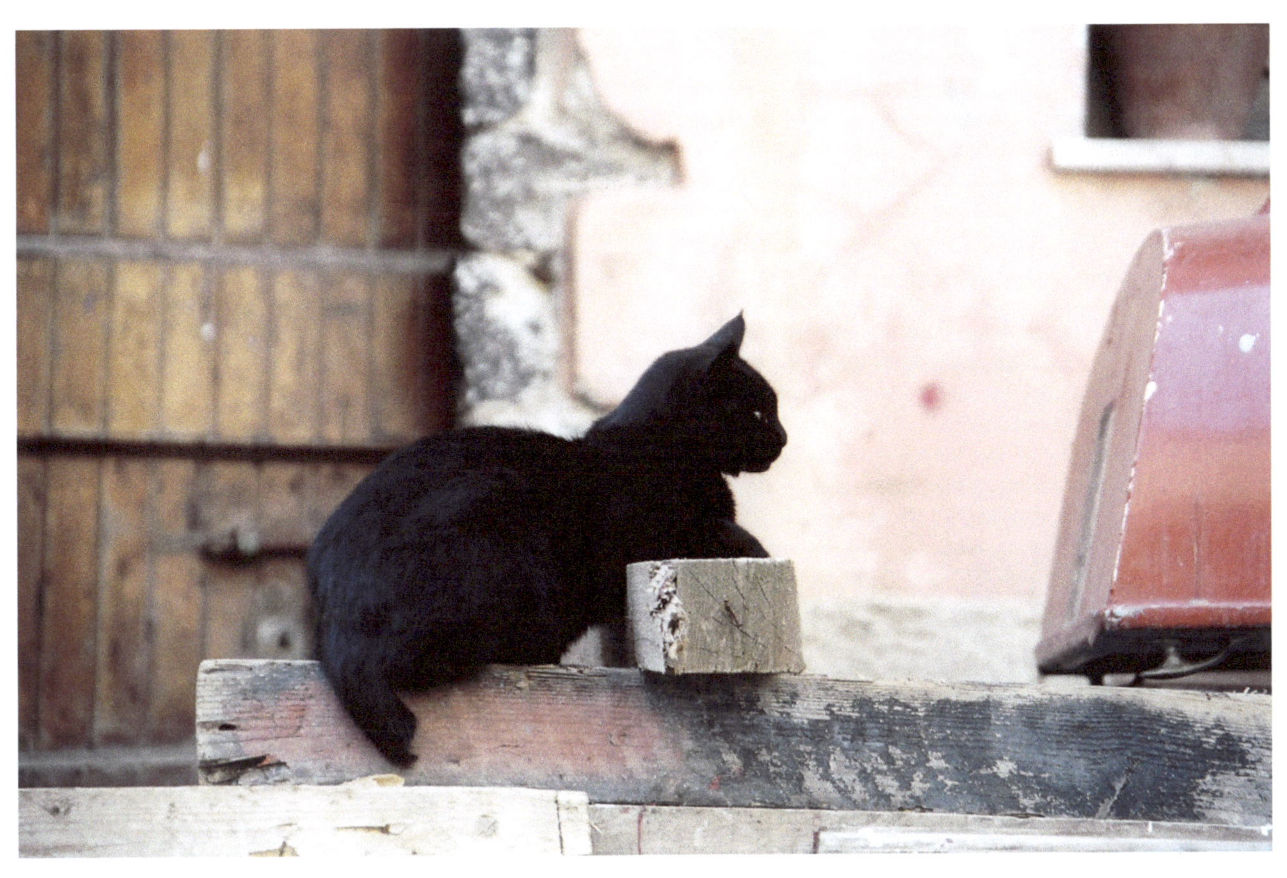

Riomaggiore, Italy

Learn what you are and be such.

--Pindar, 522-438 B.C.

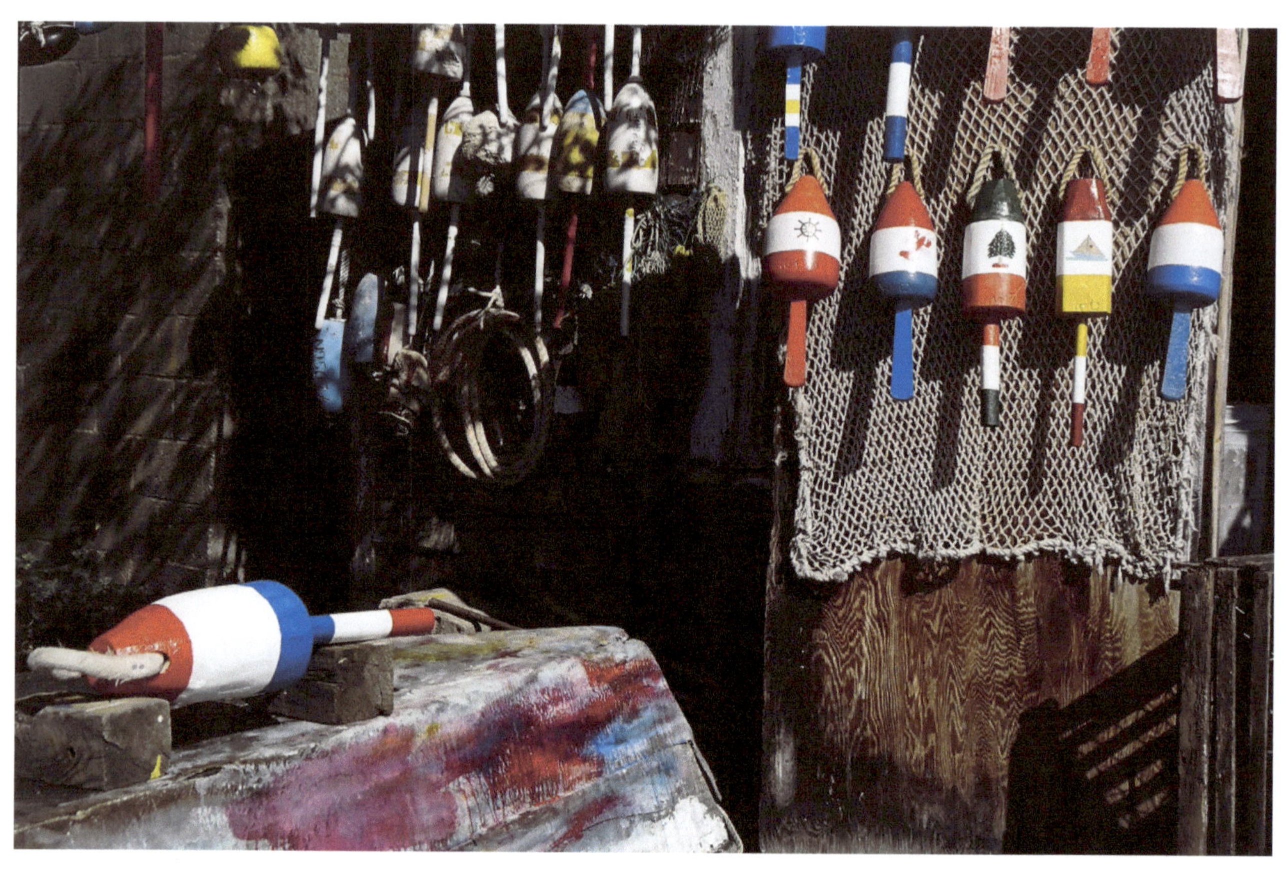

Rockport, Massachusetts

Be not angry that you cannot make others as you wish them to be,
since you cannot make yourself as you wish to be.
--Thomas a'Kempis, 1380-1472

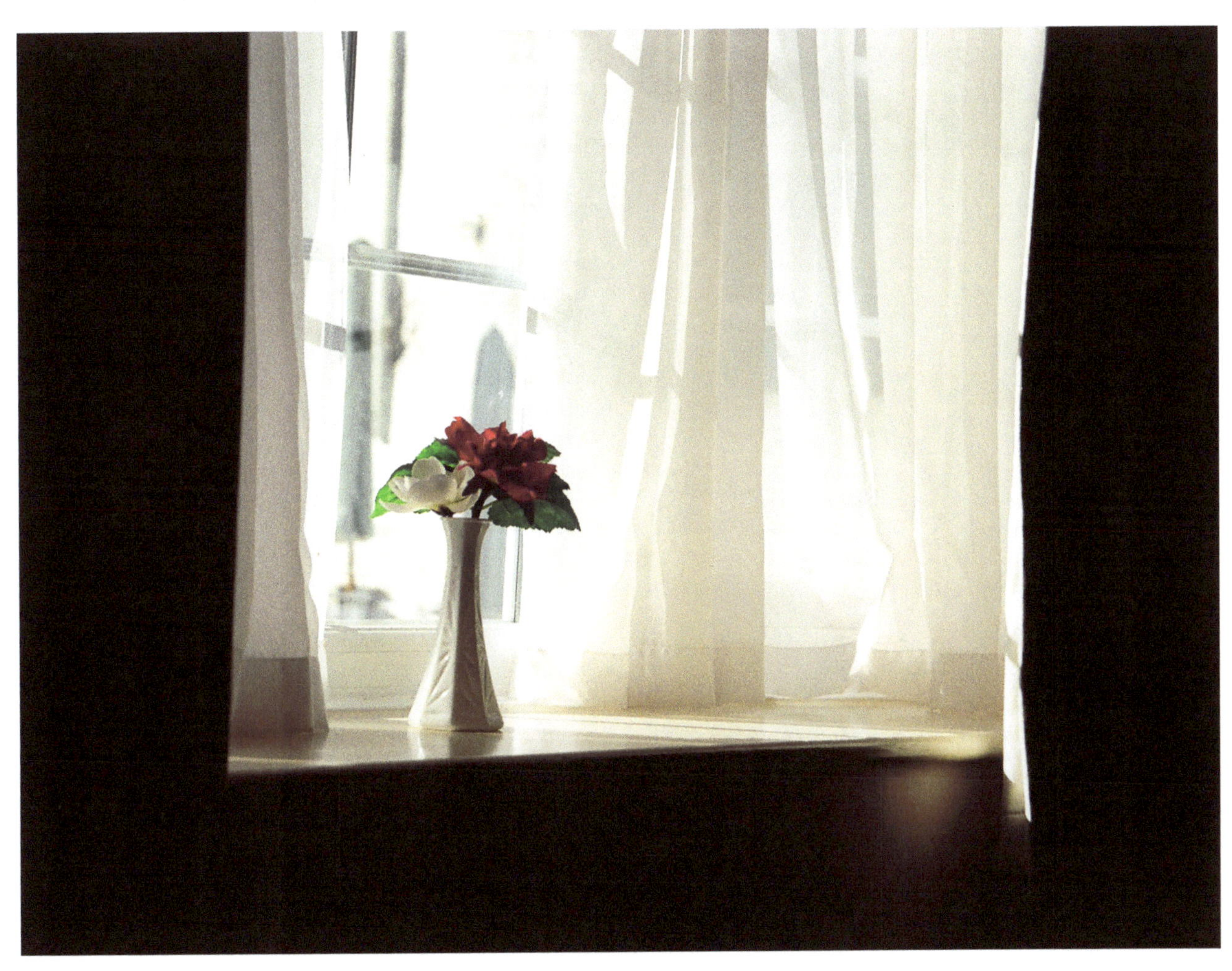

Arundel, England

We are each gifted in a unique and important way.
It is our privilege and our adventure to discover our own special light.
--Mary Dunbar, 1906-1960

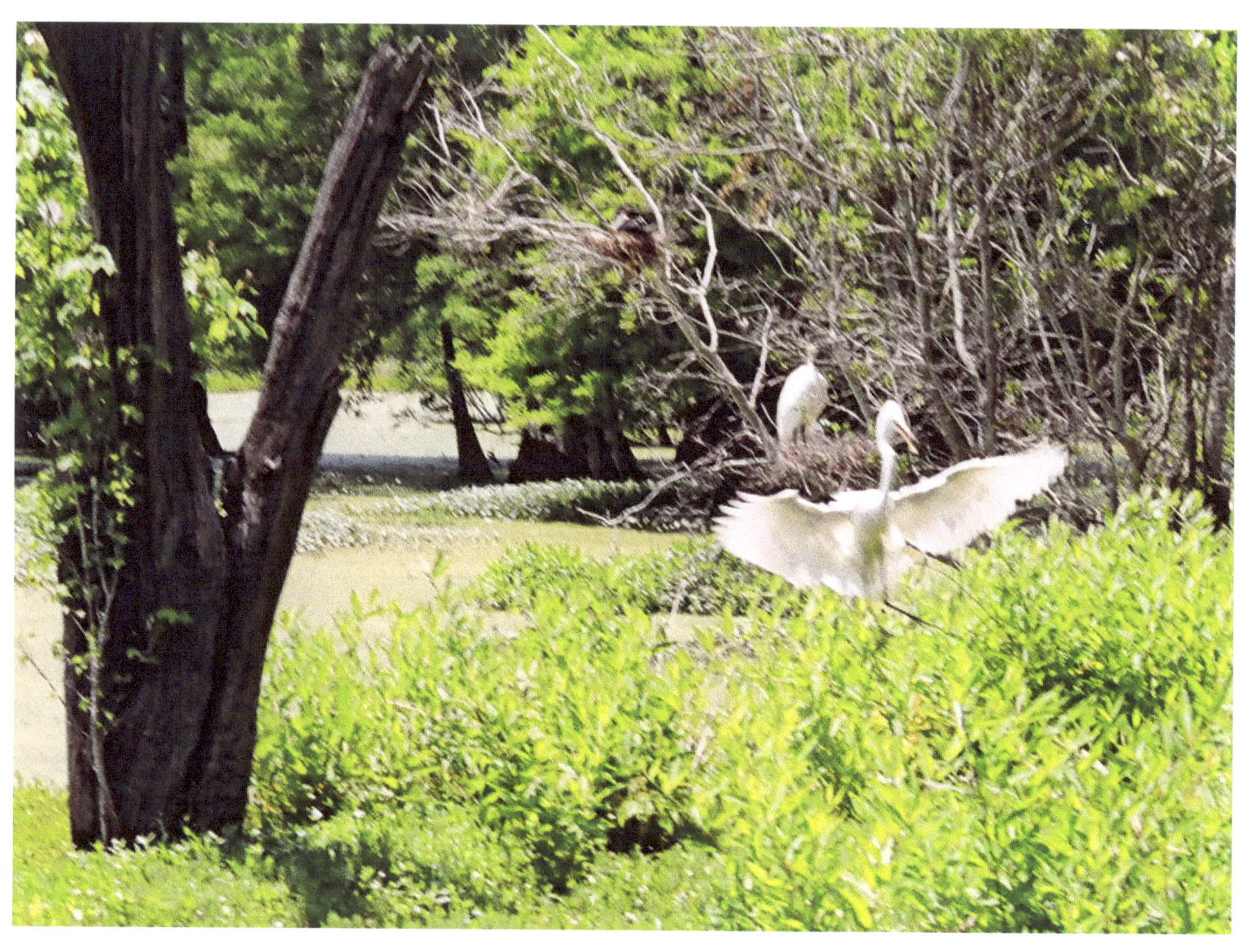

Magnolia Gardens, South Carolina

There is a need to find and sing our own song, to stretch our limbs and shake them in a dance so wild that nothing can roost there, that stirs the yearning for a solitary voyage.

--Barbara Lazear Ascher, 1946 -

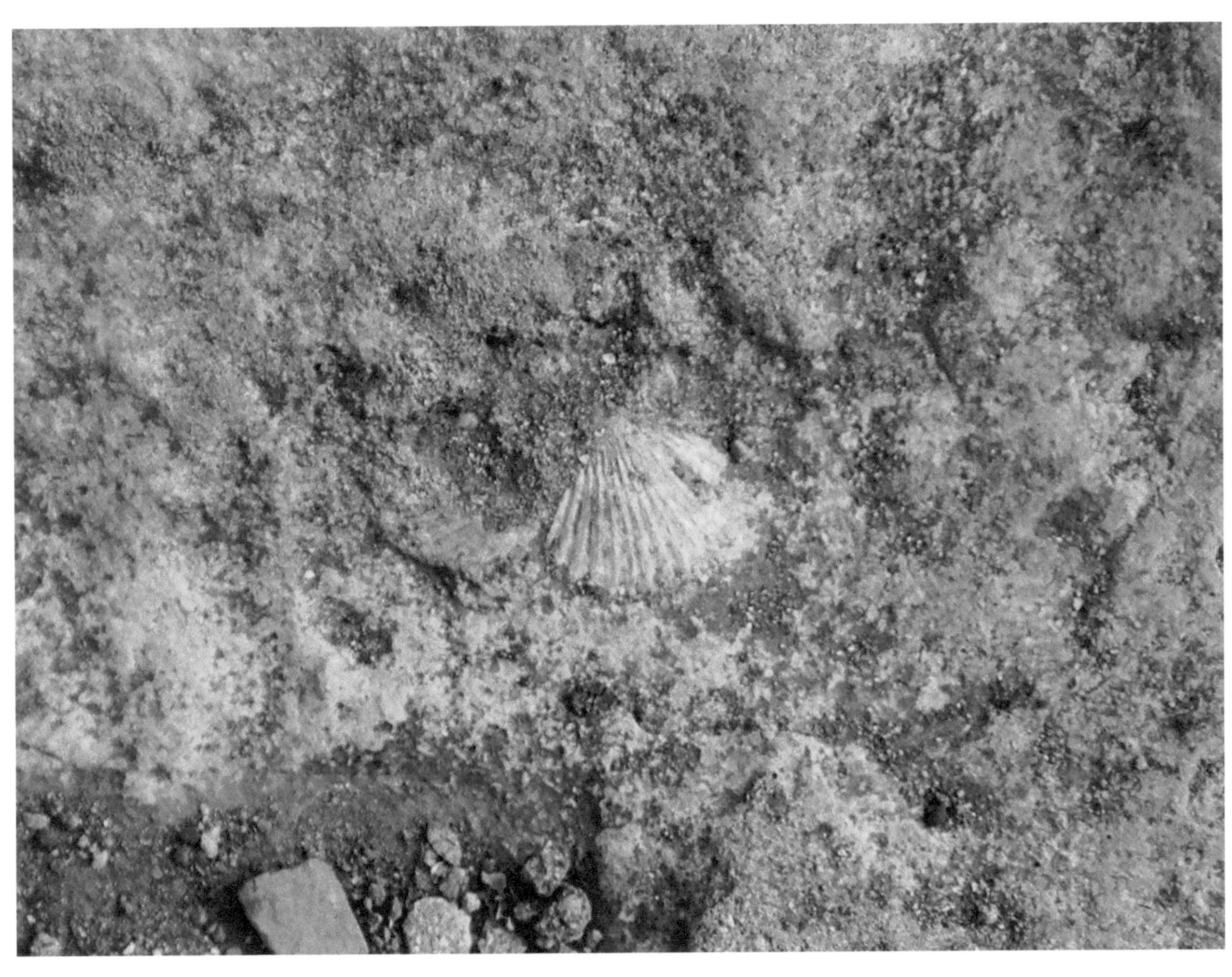

Agrigento, Sicily

Since you are like no other being ever created since the beginning of time,

you are incomparable.

--Brenda Ueland, 1891-1985

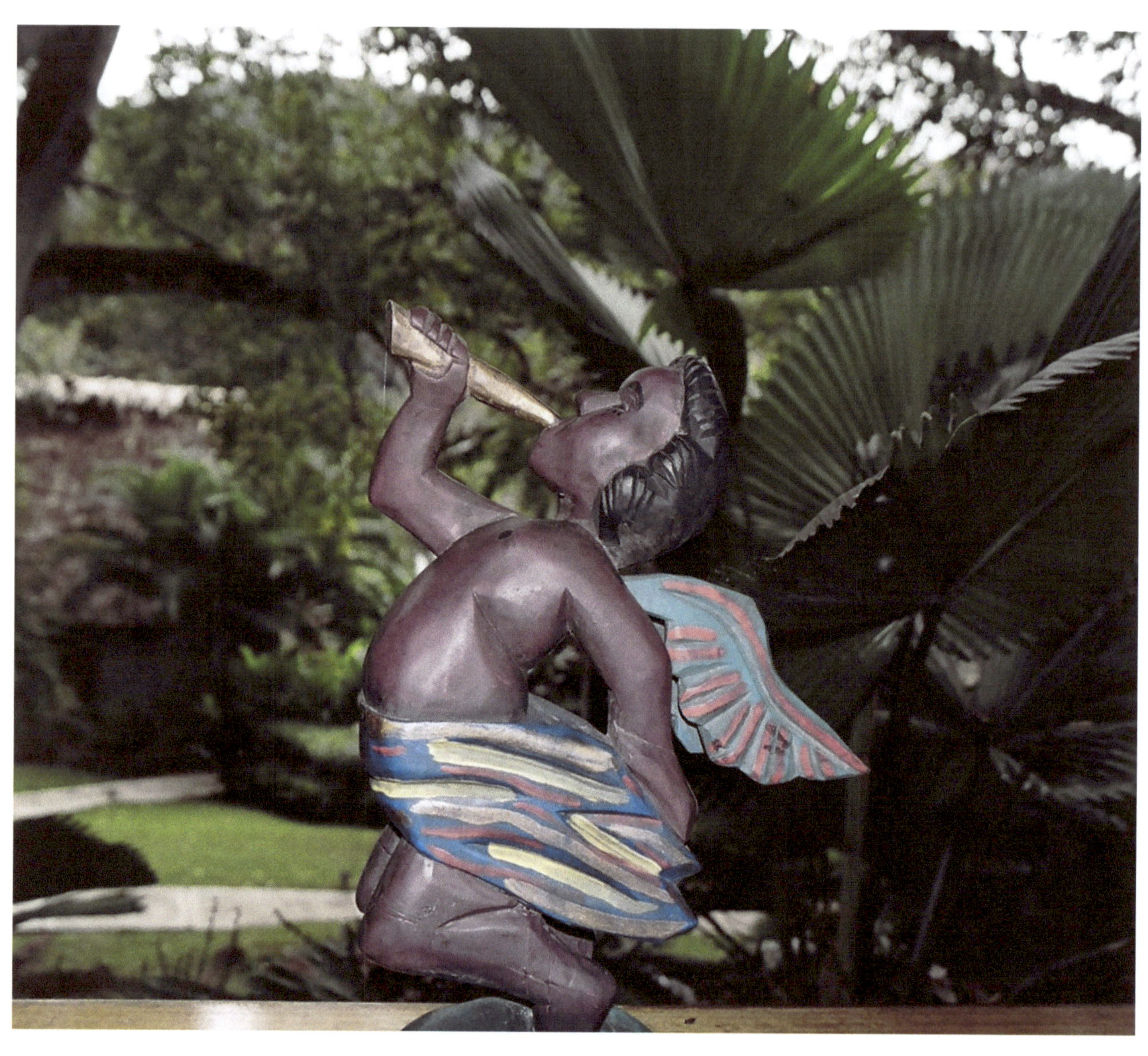

Chaa Creek, Belize

Music is your own experience, your thoughts, your wisdom.
If you don't live it, it won't come out of your horn.
--Charlie Parker, 1920-1955

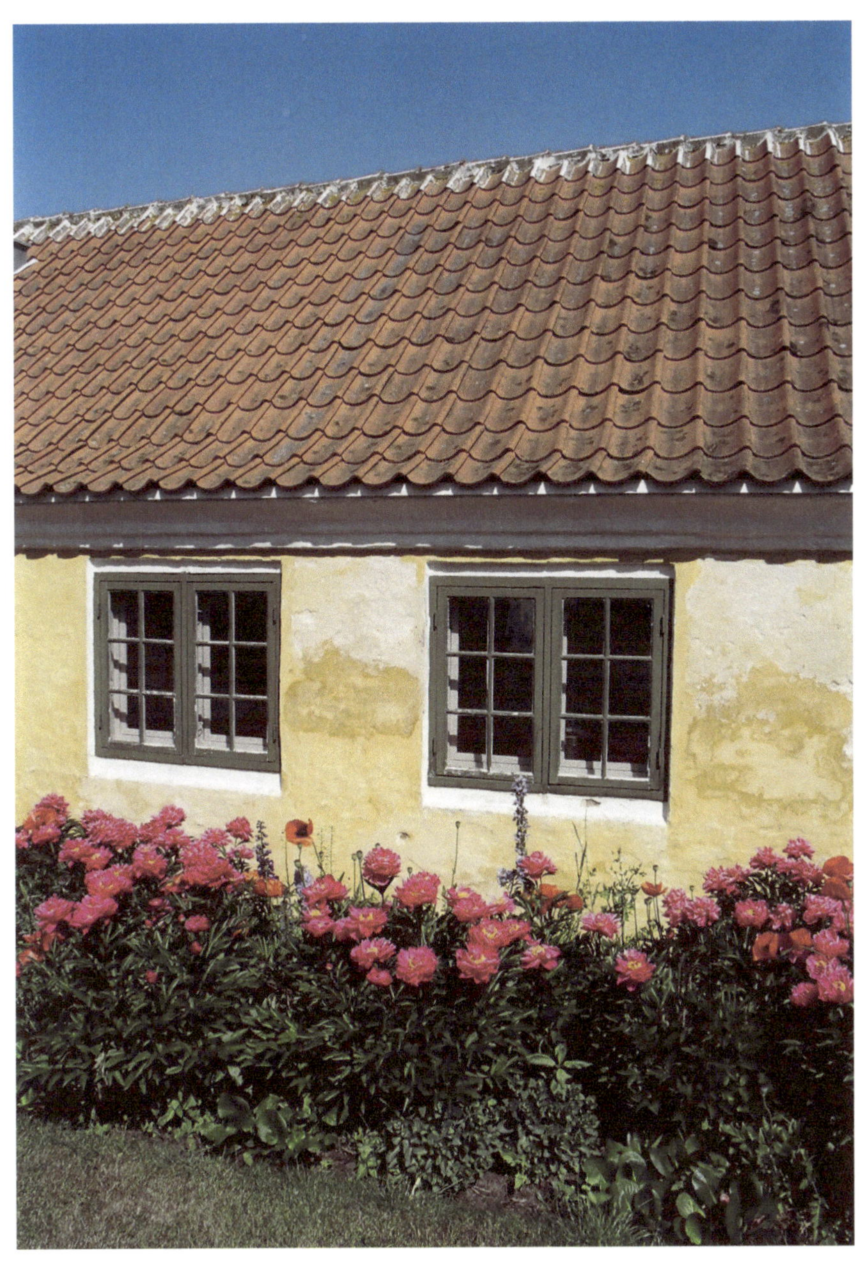

Skagen, Denmark

In search of my mother's garden I found my own.

--Alice Walker, 1944-

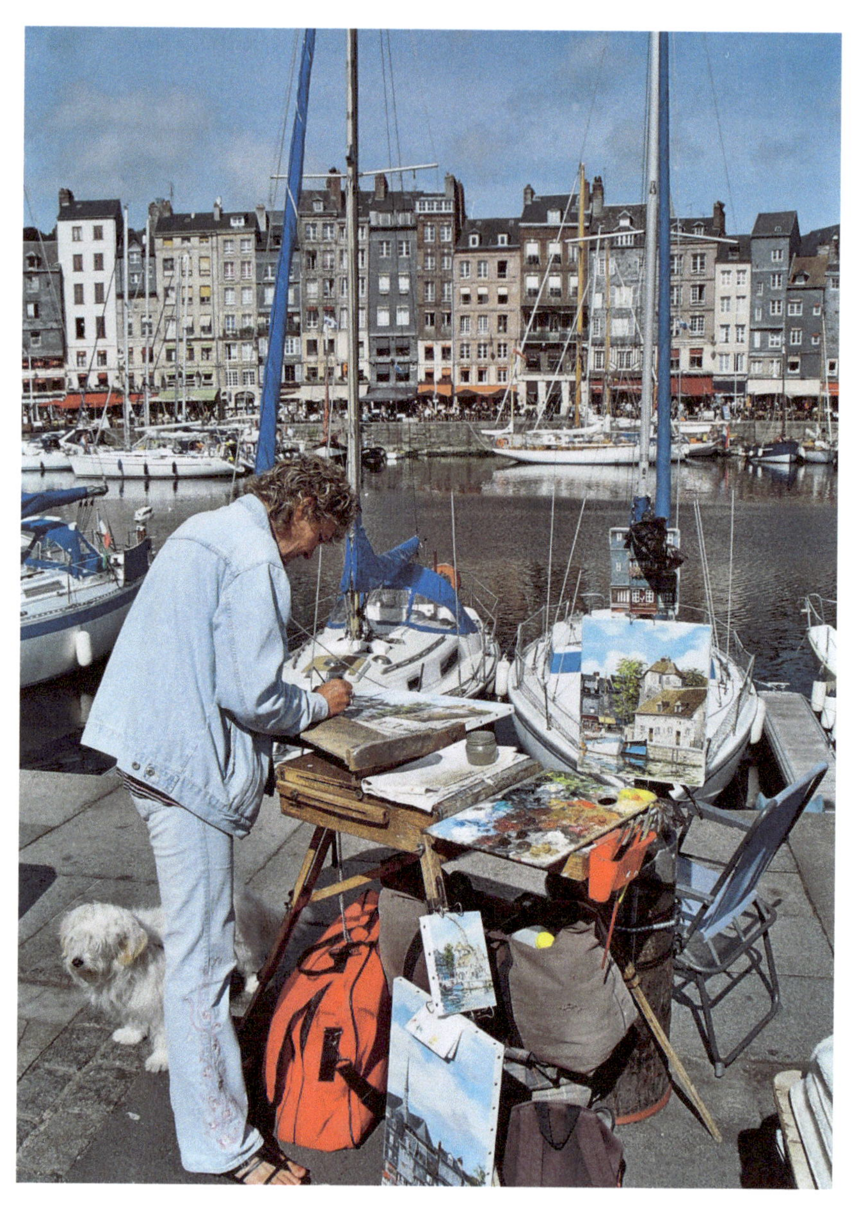

Honfleur, France

When I stand before God at the end of my life I would hope that I would not have a single bit of talent left and I can say "I used everything you gave me."

--Erma Bombeck, 1927-1996

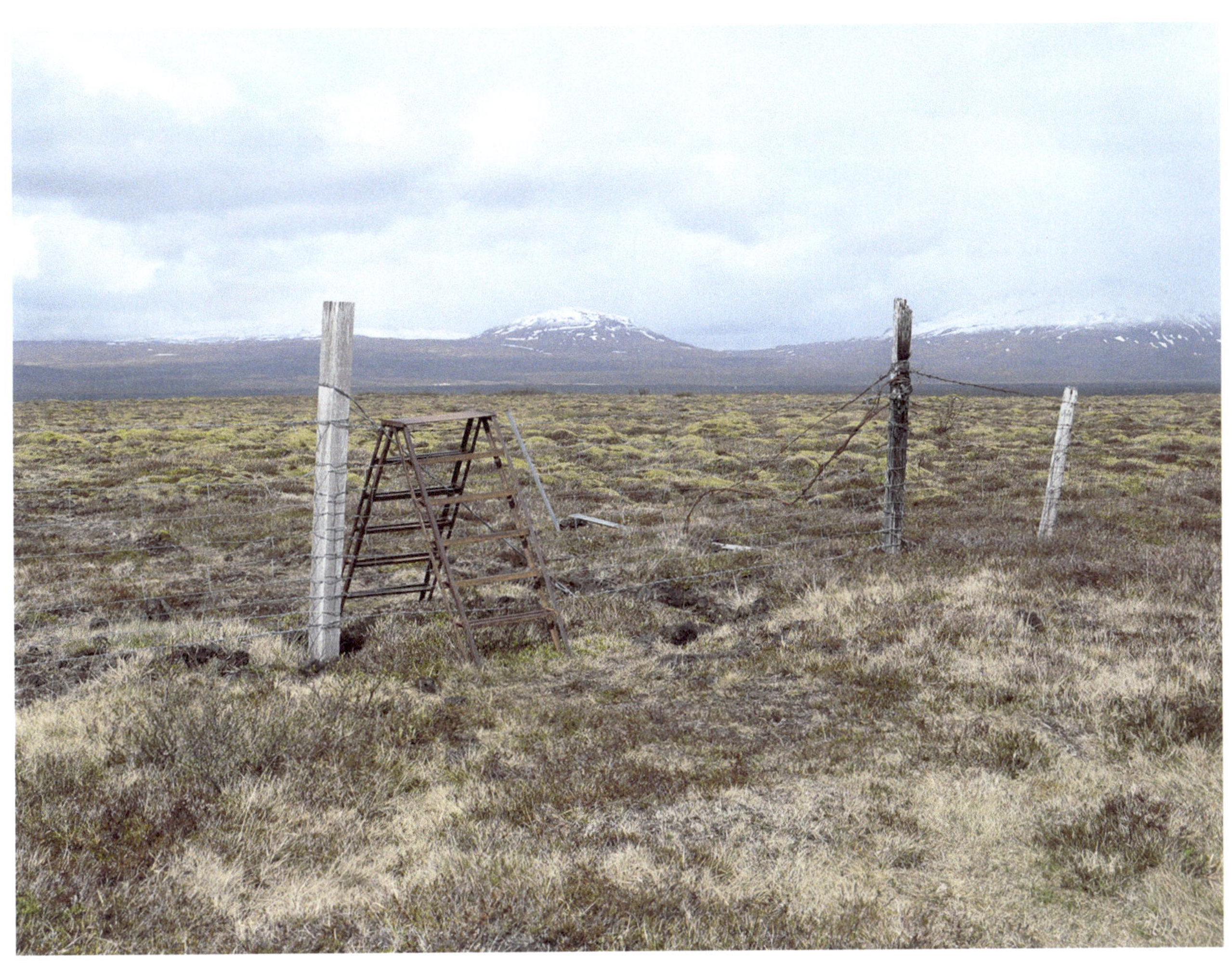

Thingvellir, Iceland

There is an internal landscape,
a geography of the soul; we search for its outlines all our lives.
– Josephine Hart

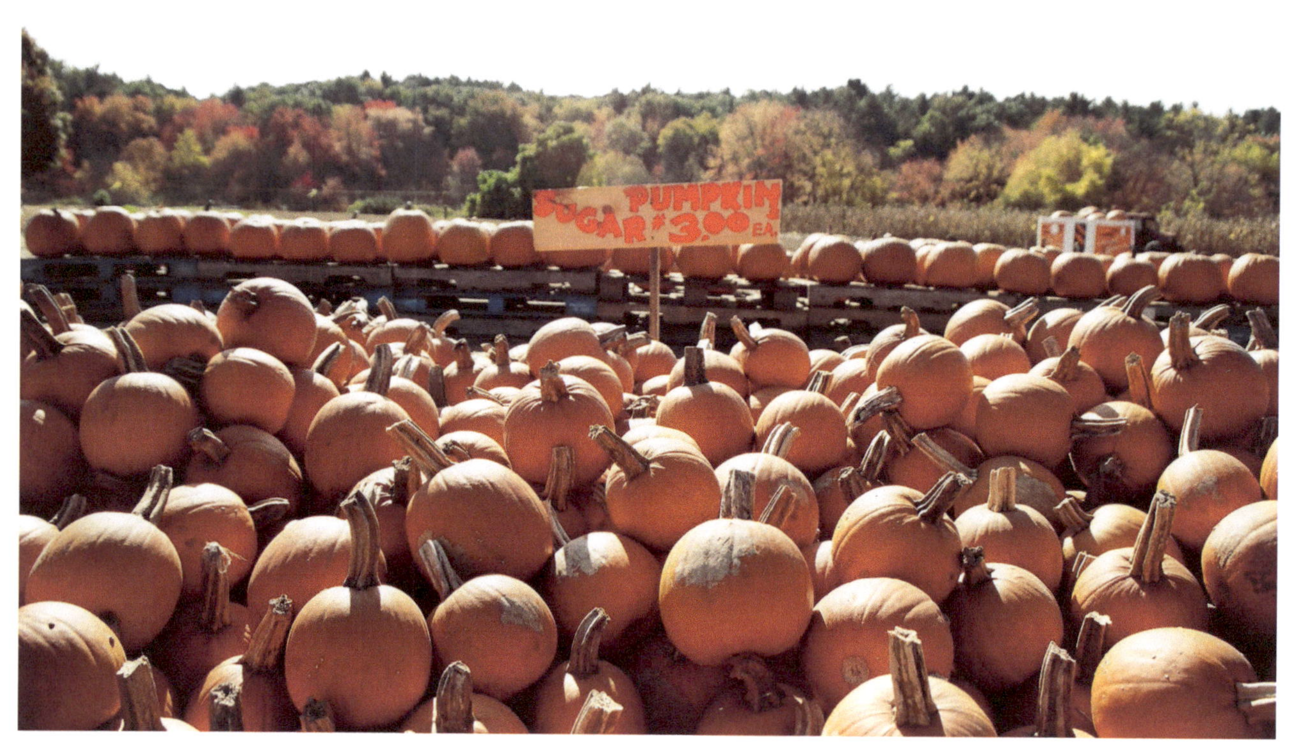

Sudbury, Massachusetts

We forfeit three-fourths of ourselves in order to be like other people.

--Arthur Schopenhauer, 1788-1860

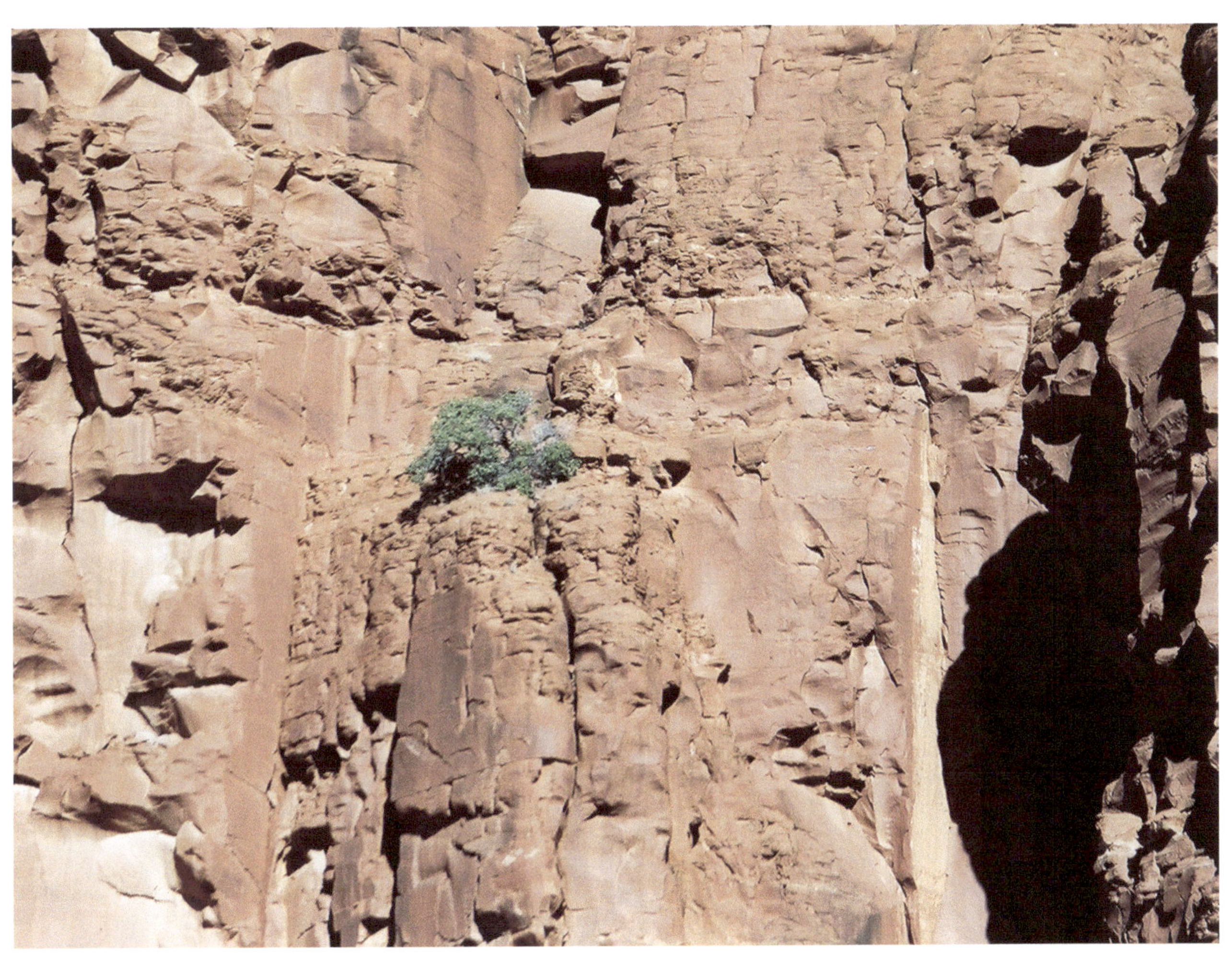

Cathedral Rock, Arizona

We are made to persist.
That's how we find out who we are.
--Tobias Wolff, 1945-

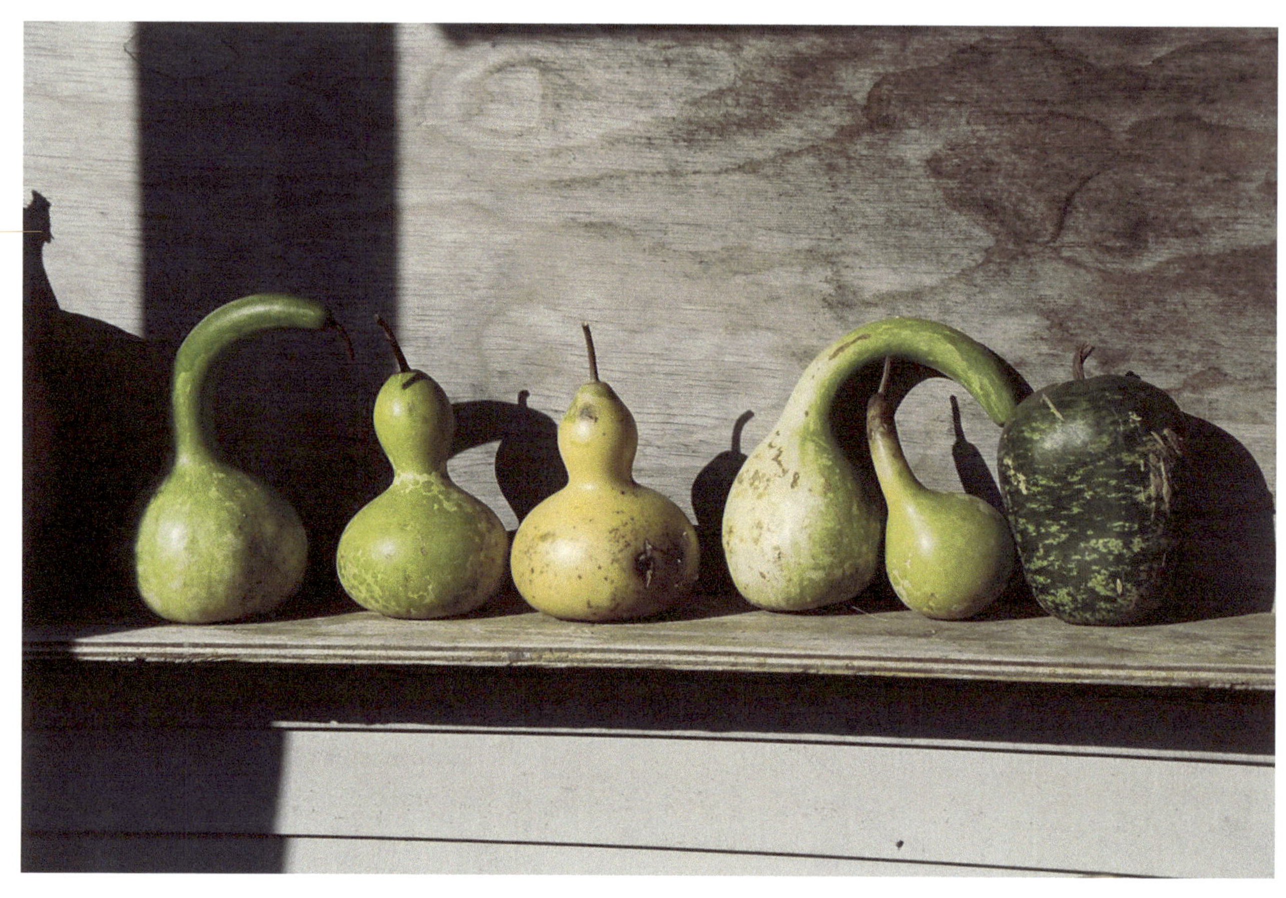

Southern Vermont

Be a first rate version of yourself,
not a second rate version of someone else.
--Judy Garland, 1922-1969

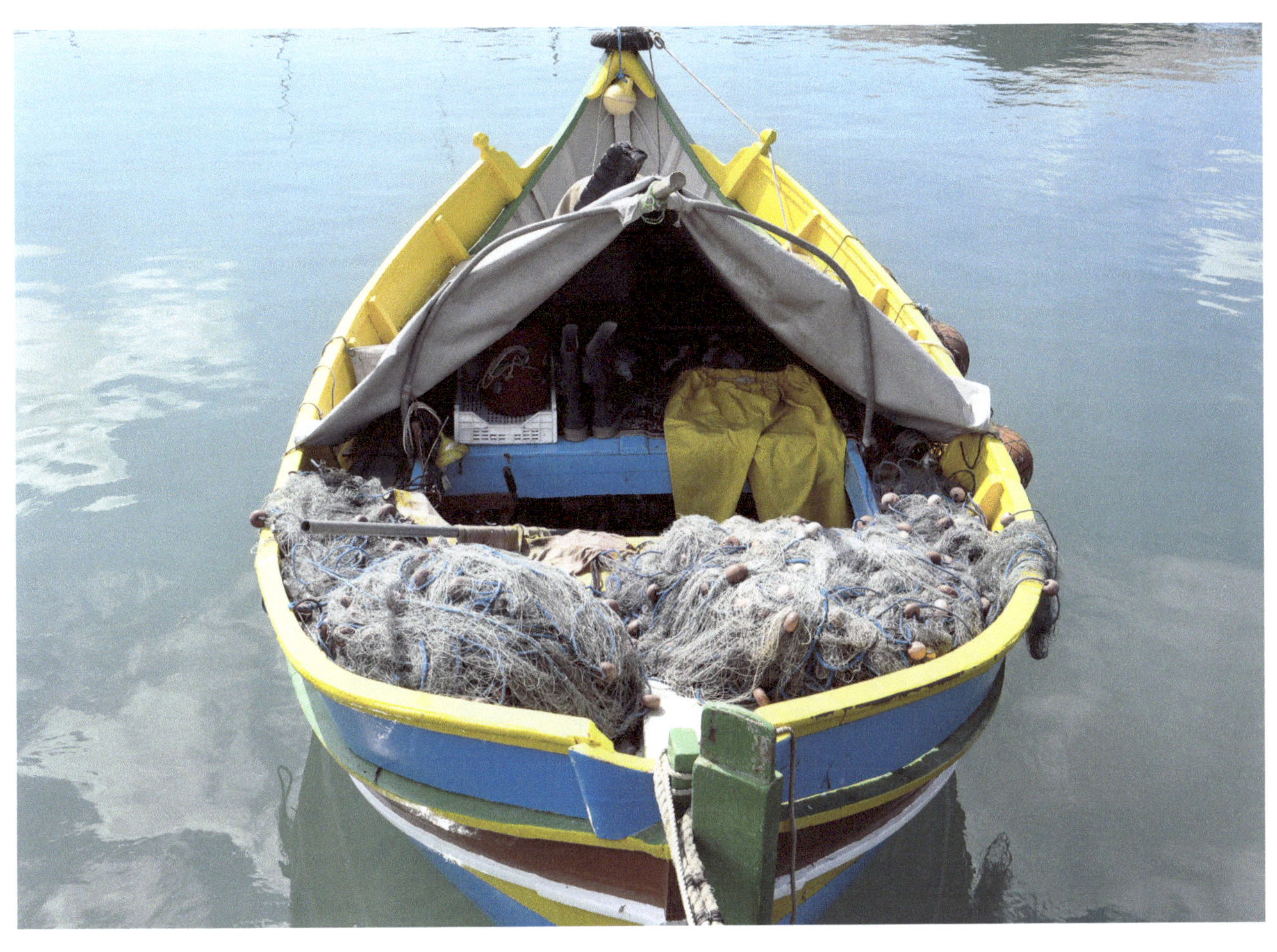

Marsaxlokk Bay, Malta

There is just one life for each of us: our own.

--Euripides, 485-406 B.C.

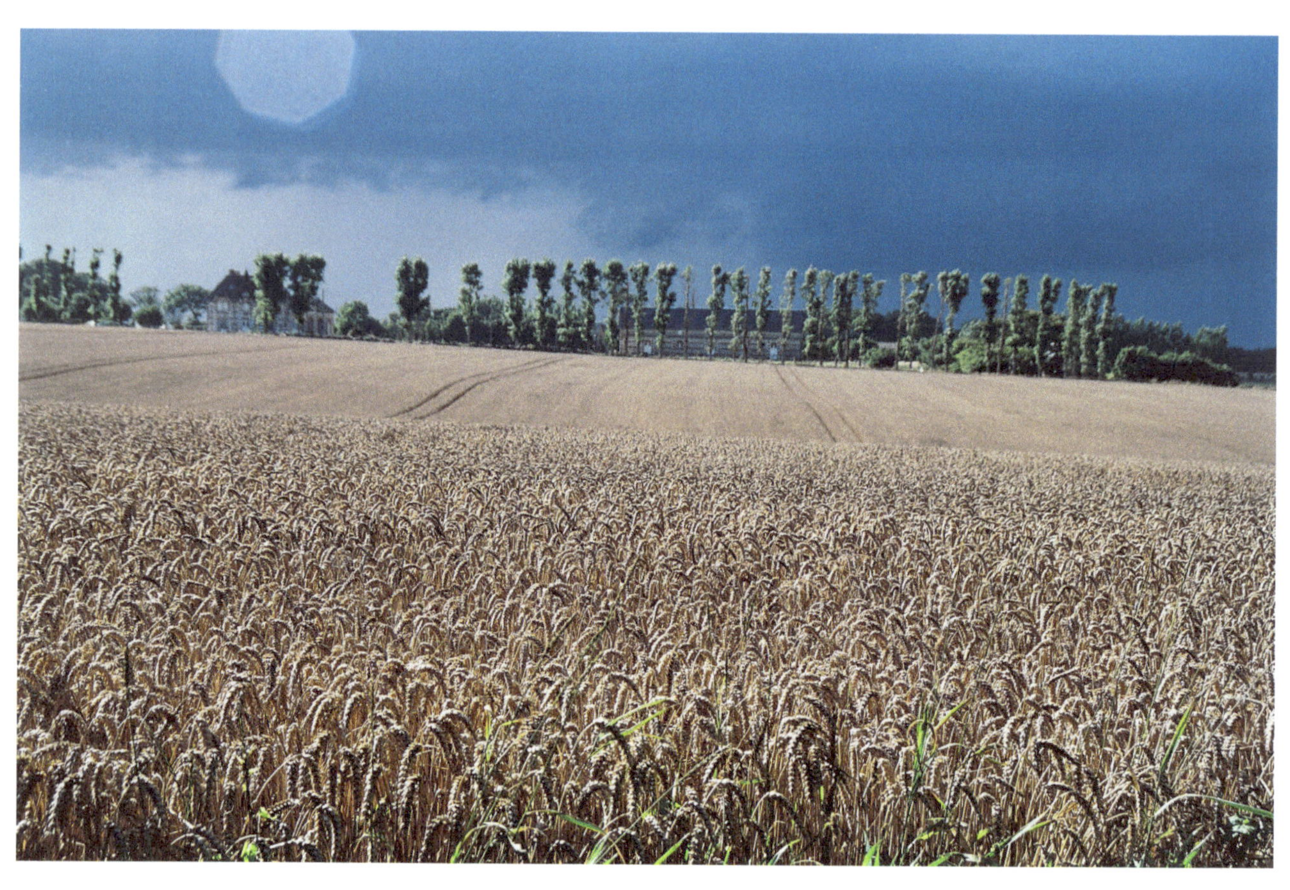

Normandy, France

You don't need a weatherman to know which way the wind blows.

--Bob Dylan, 1941-

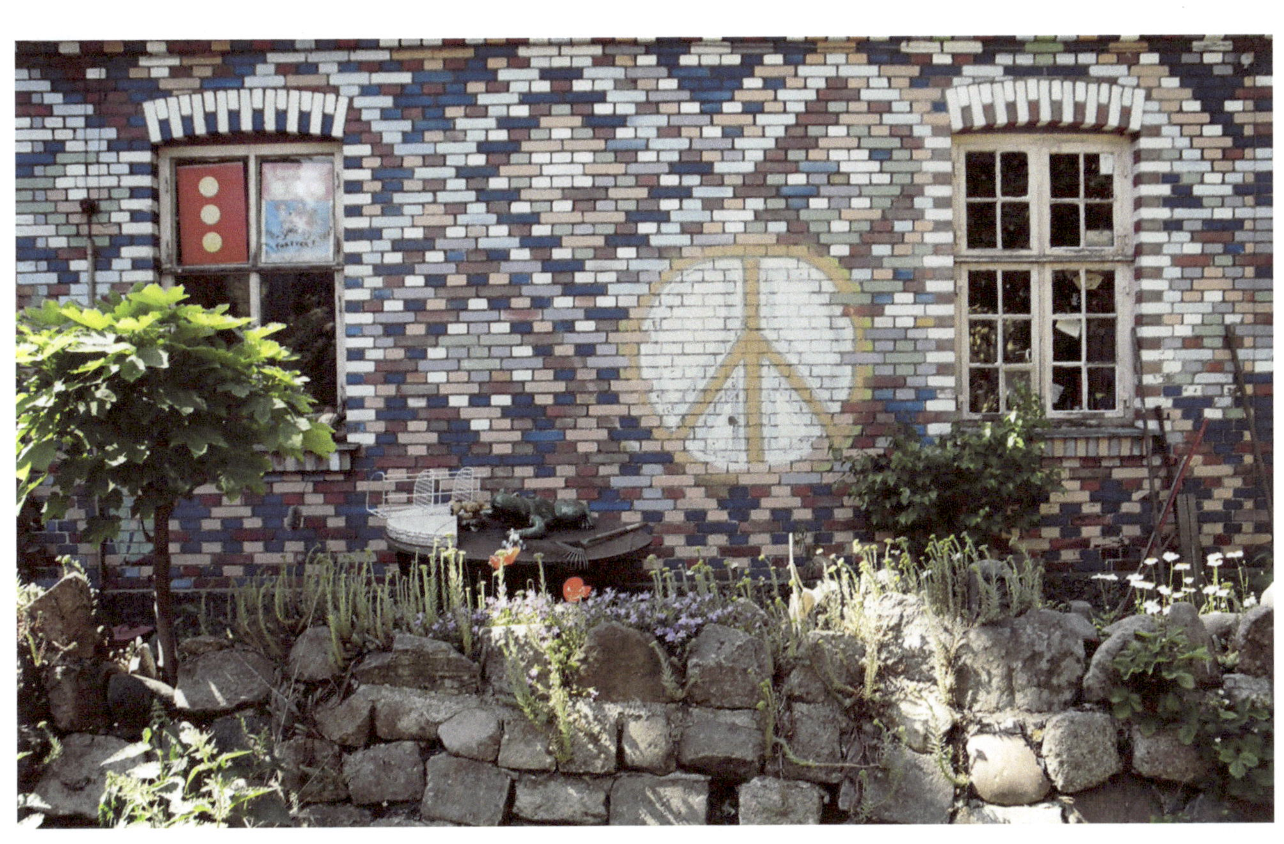

Christiania, Denmark

Until you make peace with who you are,

you'll never be content with what you have.

--Doris Mortman, 1945-

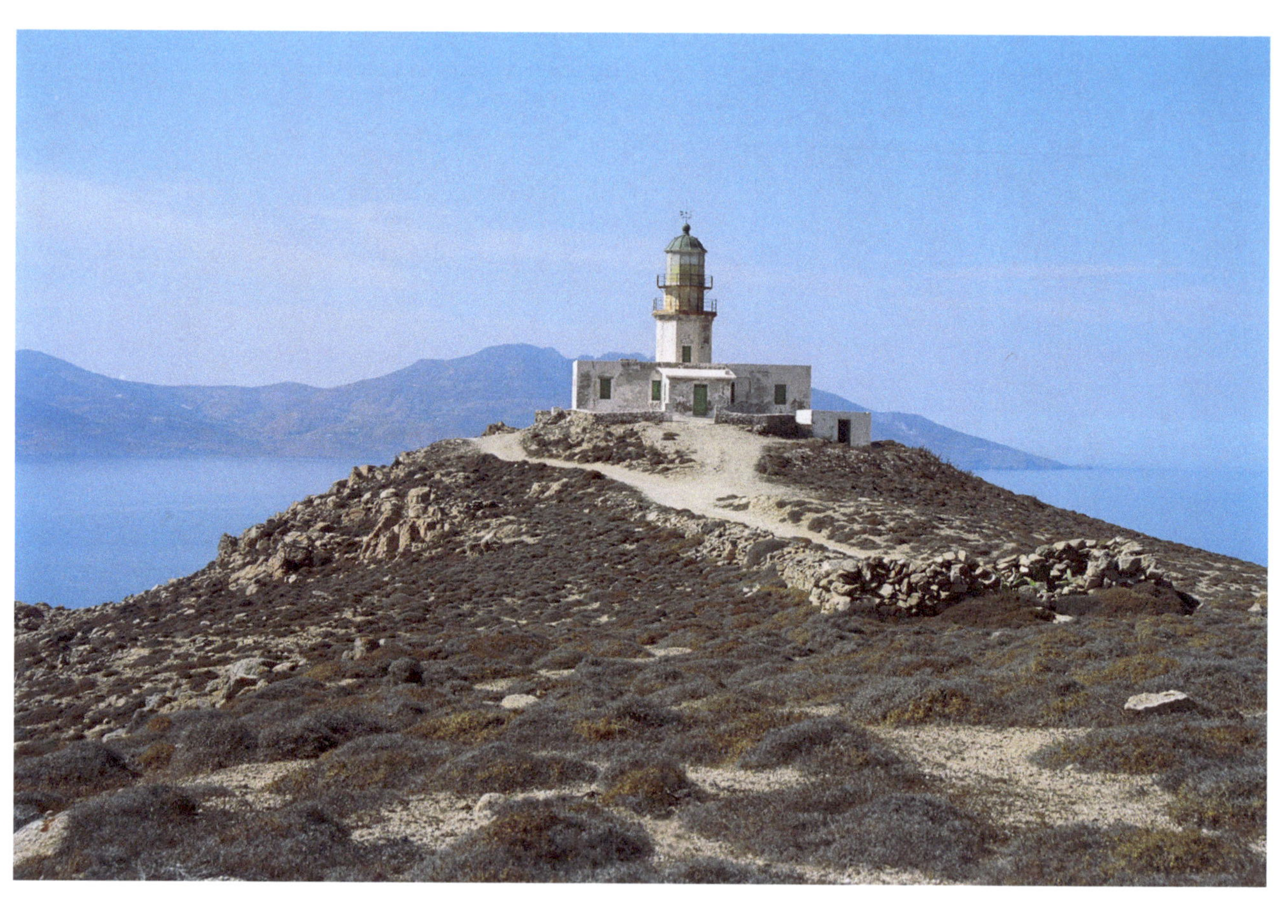

Mykonos, Greece

When your soul quits taking refuge in the pretenses and stops being a fugitive from Spirit,
it will catch on fire and serve as a beacon lighting the way to
your calling, your destiny, to being completely and entirely you.
--John Renesch

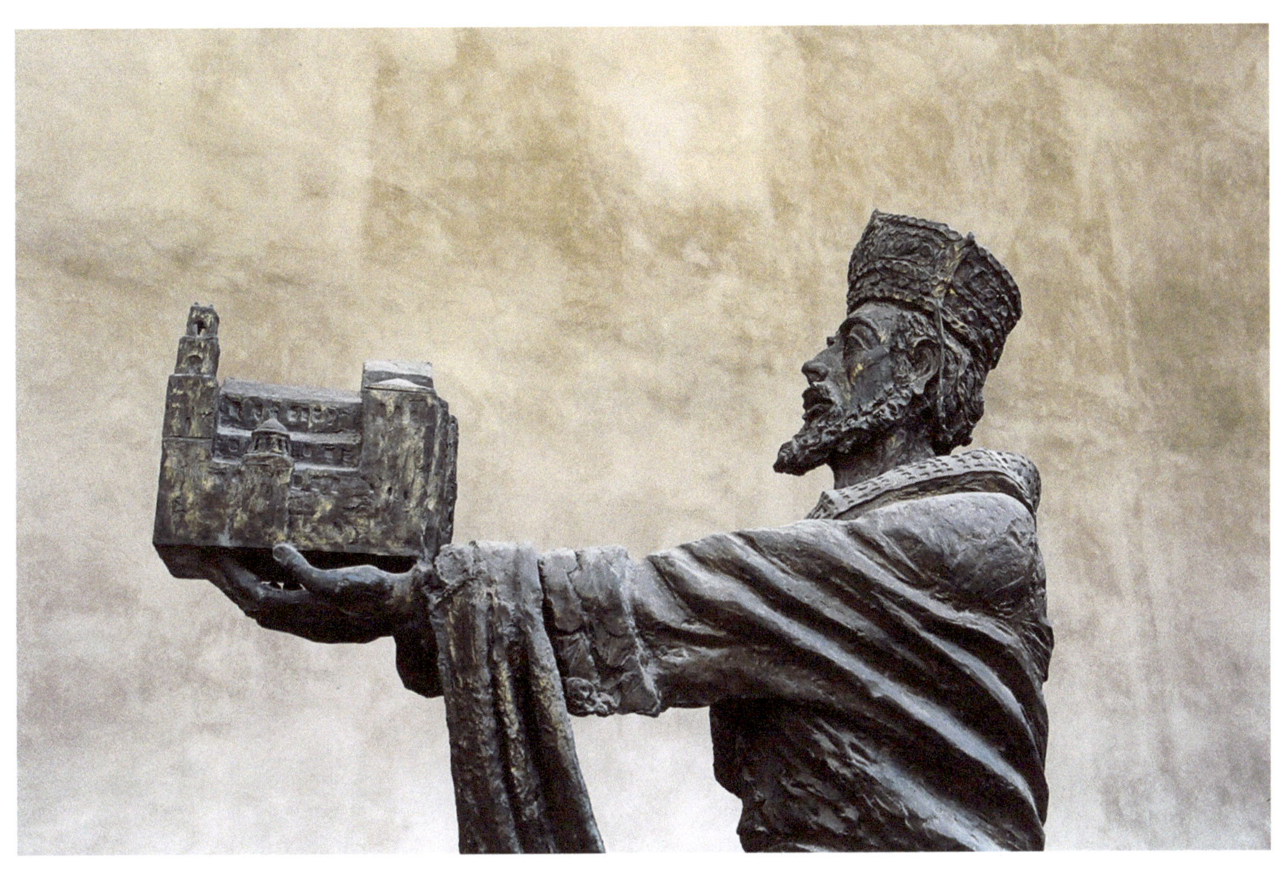

Monreale, Sicily

We never know how high we are till we are called to rise
And then, if we are true to plan, our statures touch the skies.
--Emily Dickinson, 1830-1886

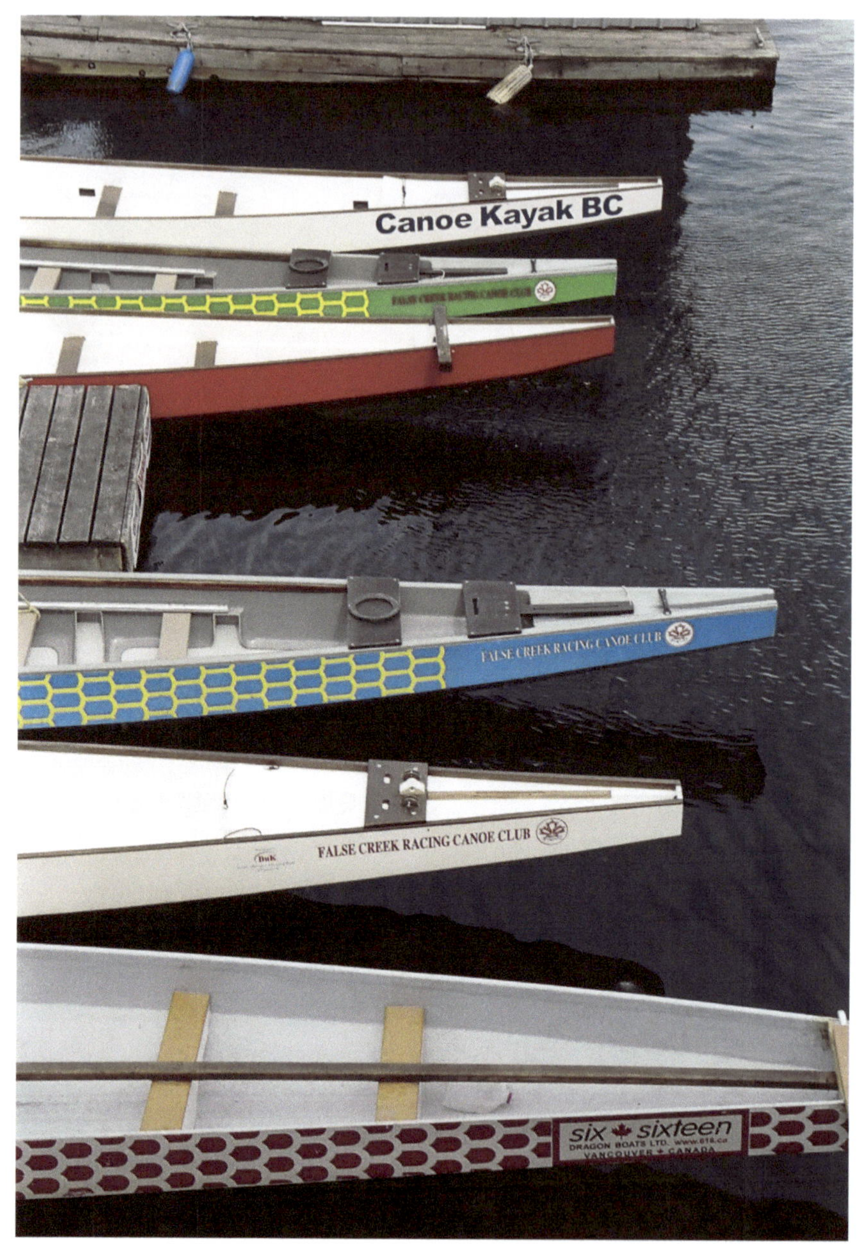

False Creek, British Columbia

I am as bad as the worst, but, thank God,

I am as good as the best.

--Walt Whitman, 1819-1892

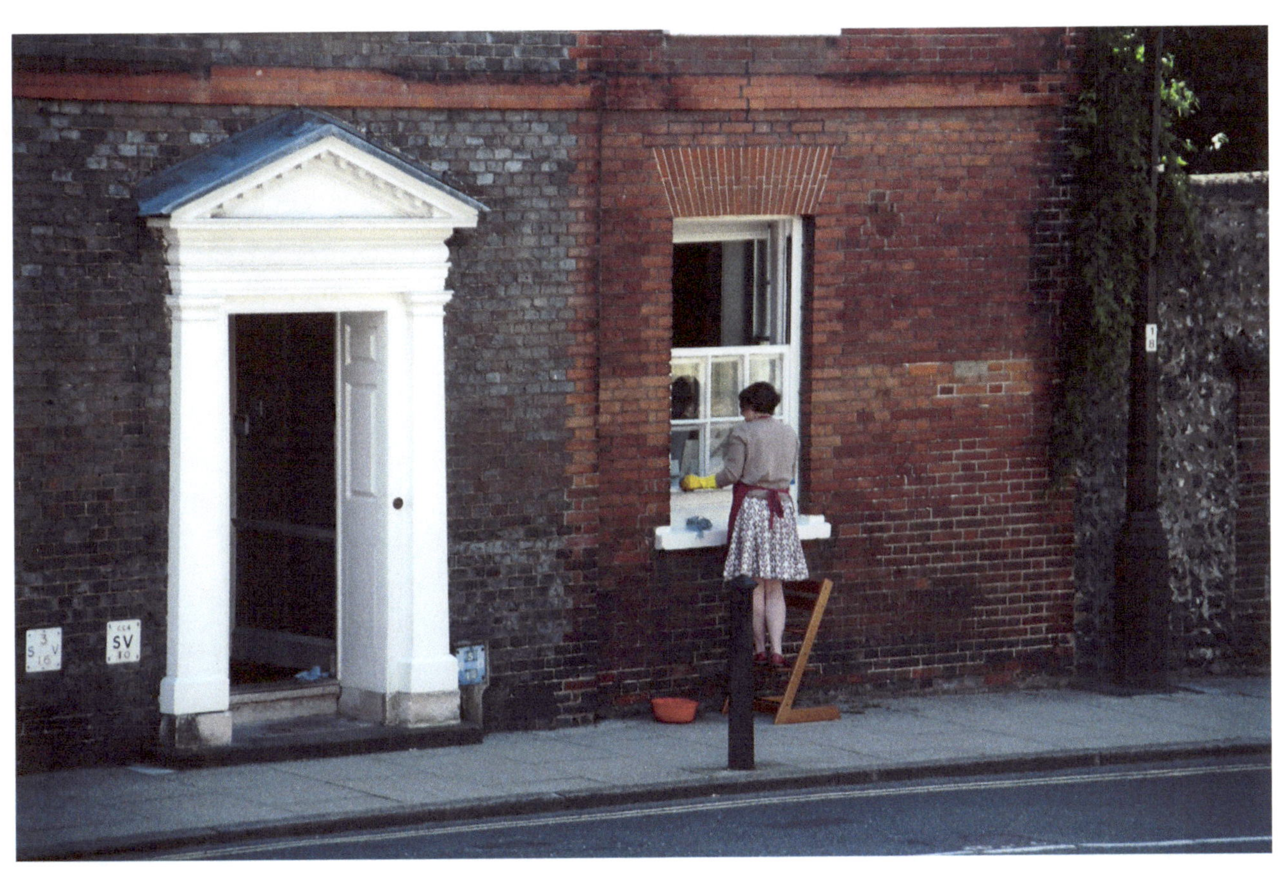

Arundel, England

For the meaning of life differs from man to man,
from day to day, from hour to hour.
What matters, therefore, is not the meaning of life in general
but rather the specific meaning at a given moment.
--Viktor Frankl, 1905-1997

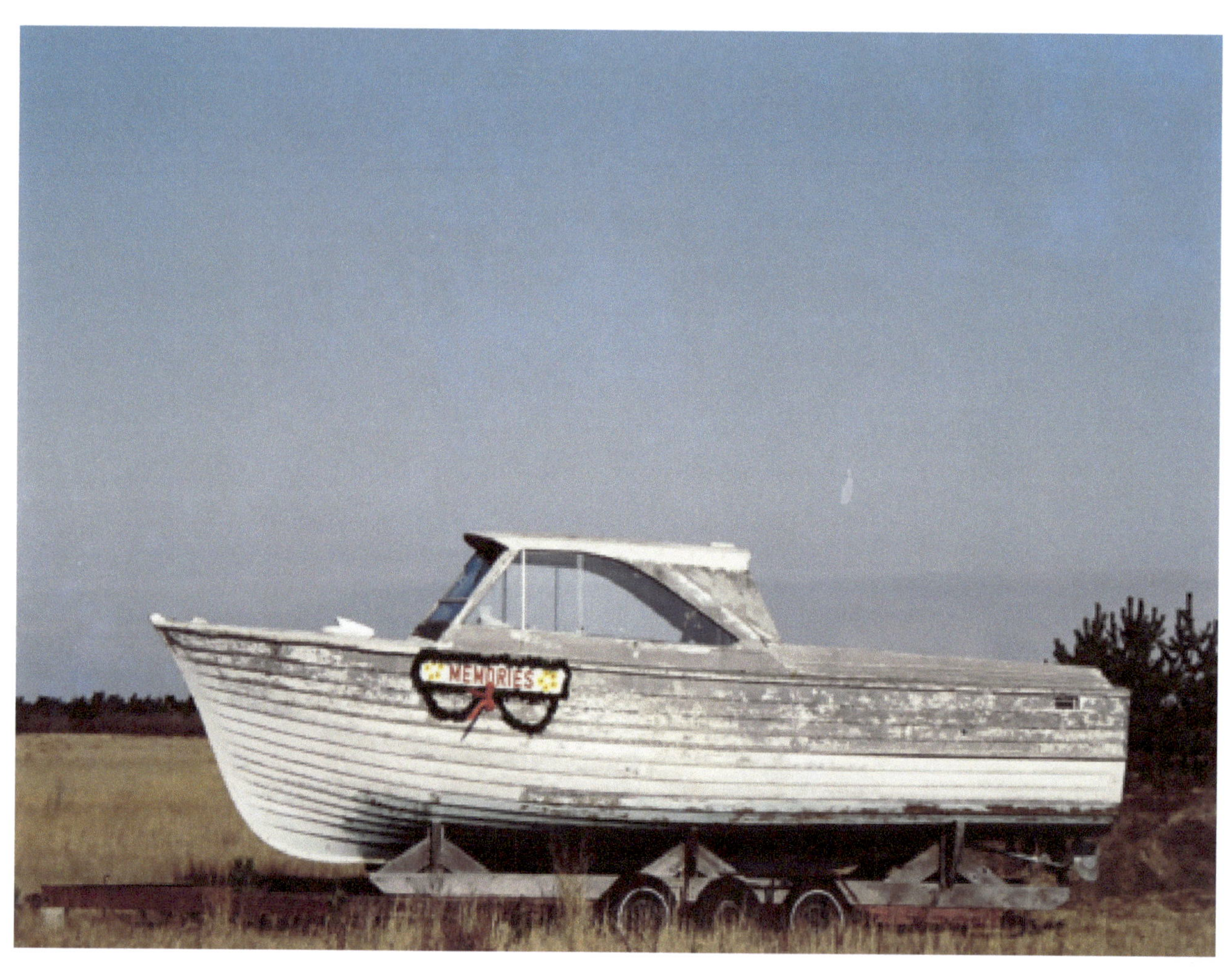

Nantucket, Massachusetts

In the depth of winter,

I finally learned that within me there lay an invincible summer.

--Albert Camus, 1913-1960

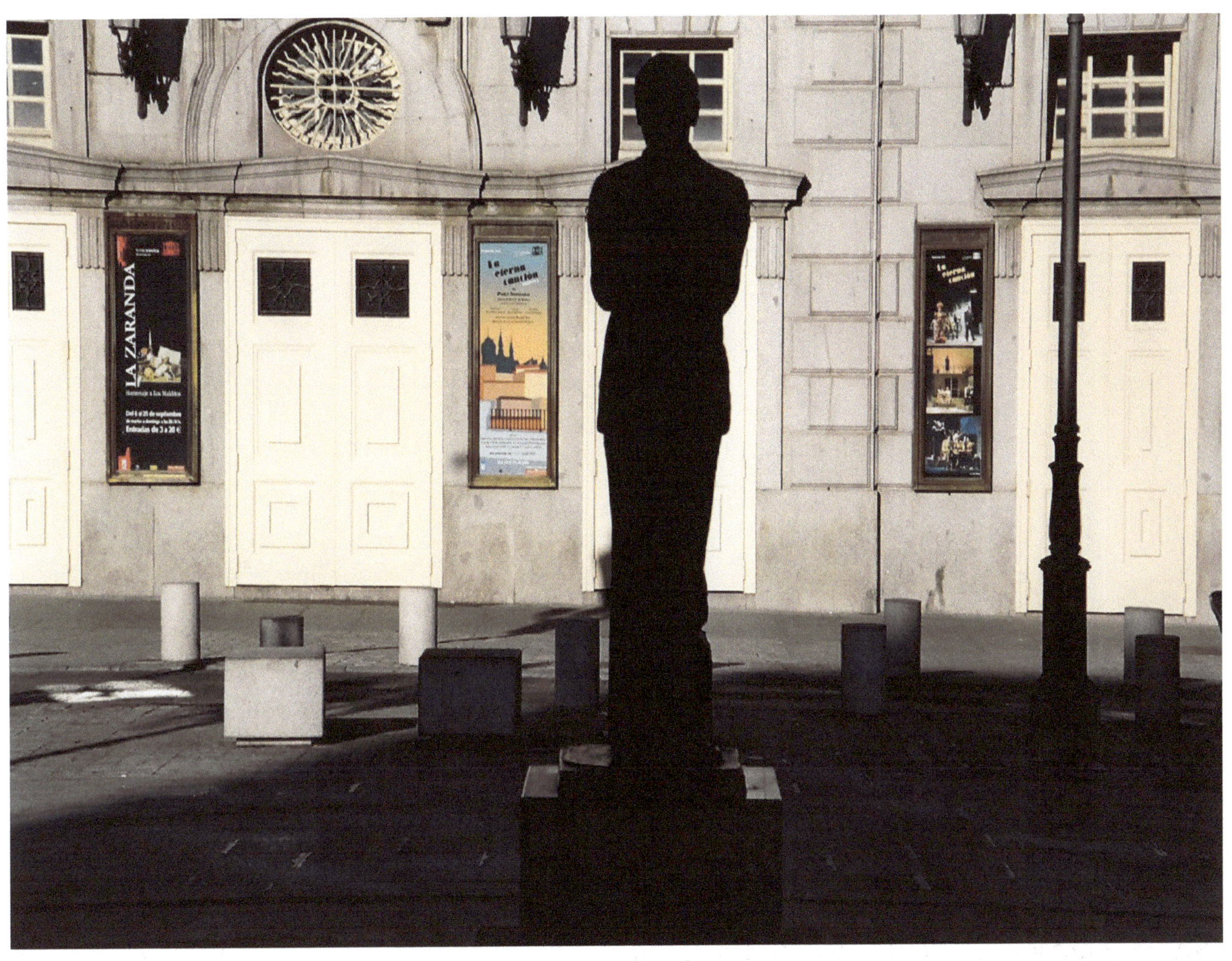

Madrid, Spain

No more important duty can be urged upon those who are entering the great theatre of life than simple loyalty to their best convictions.
--Edwin Hubbel Chapin, 1814- 1880

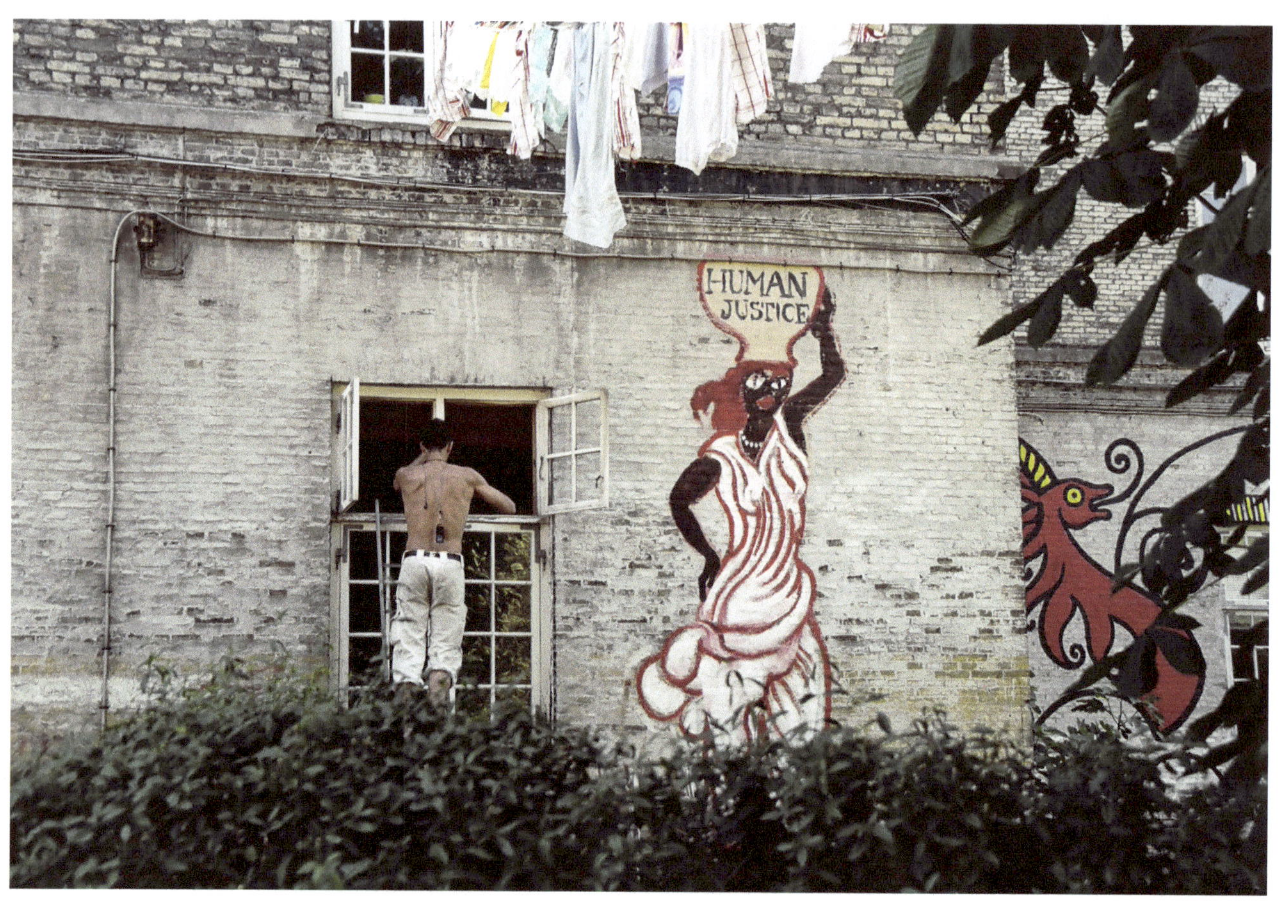

Christiania, Denmark

Only he is free who cultivates his own thoughts,

and strives without fear to do justice to them.

--Berthold Auerbach, 1812-1882

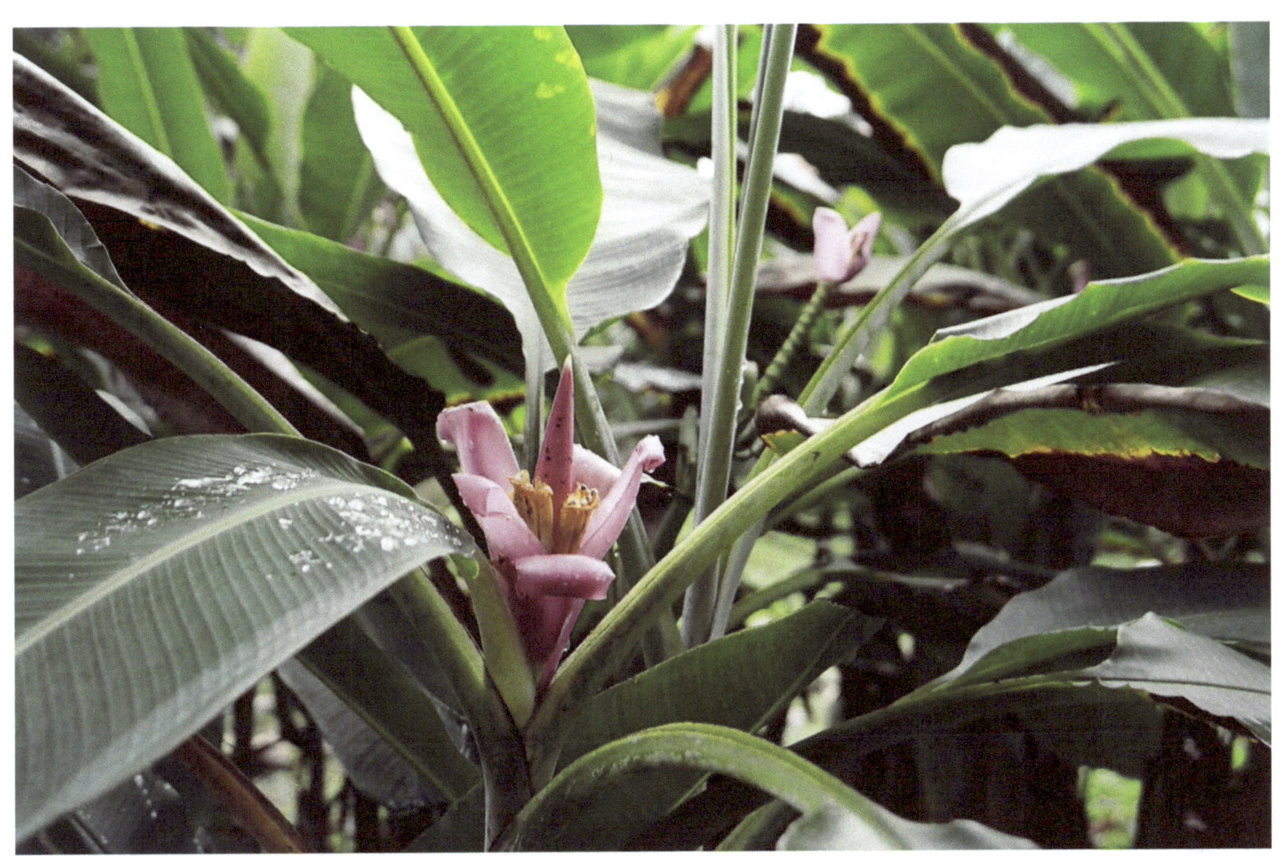

Chaa Creek, Belize

And the day came when the risk it took to remain tight inside the bud
was more painful than the risk it took to blossom.

--Anais Nin, 1903-1977

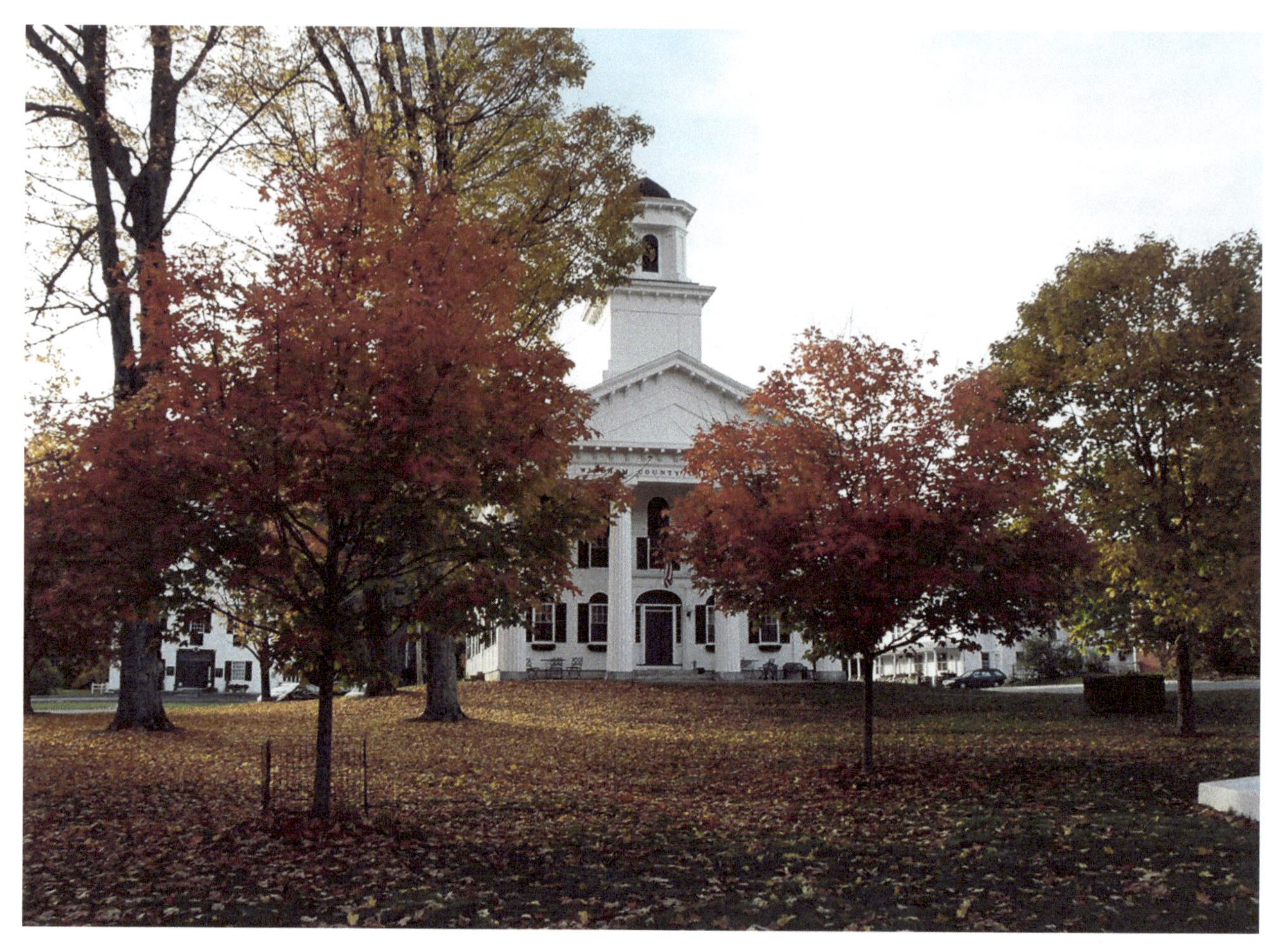

Southern Vermont

I do not accept any absolute formulas for living.
No preconceived code can see ahead to everything that can happen in a man's life.
As we live, we grow and our beliefs change.
--Martin Buber, 1878-1965

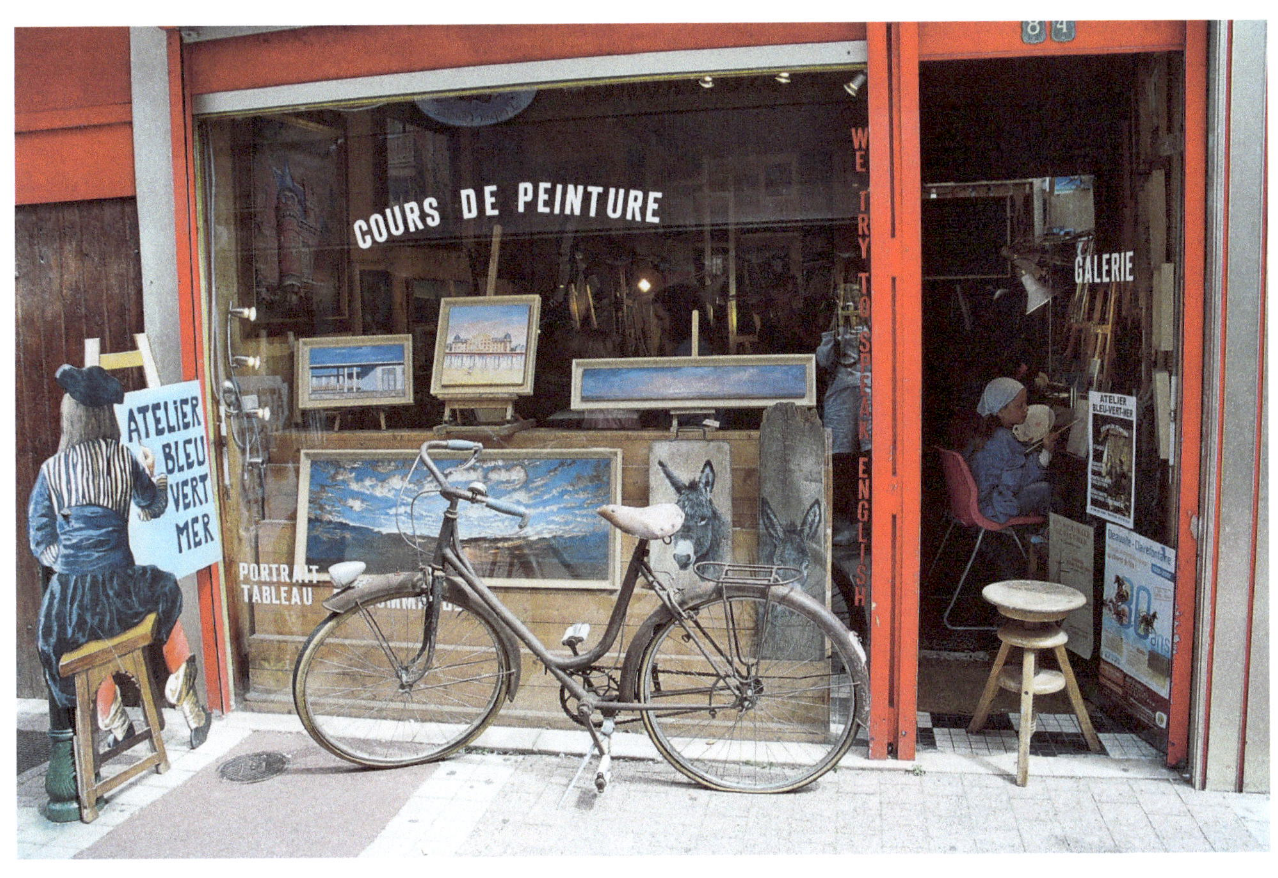

Trouville, France

Every child is an artist.

The problem is to remain an artist once you grow up.

--Pablo Picasso, 1881-1973

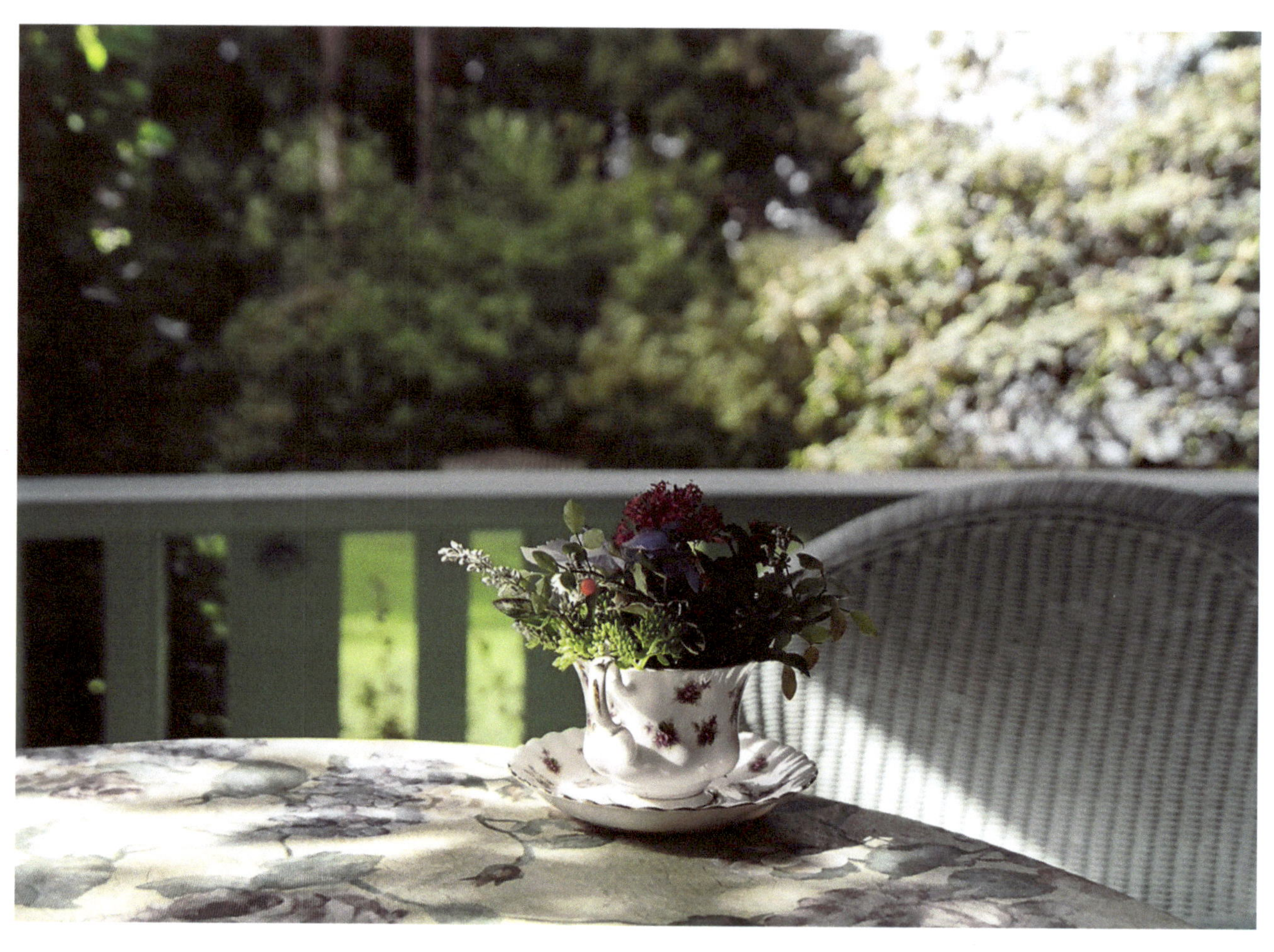

Milner Gardens, British Columbia

May you learn to be a good friend to yourself.
--Irish blessing

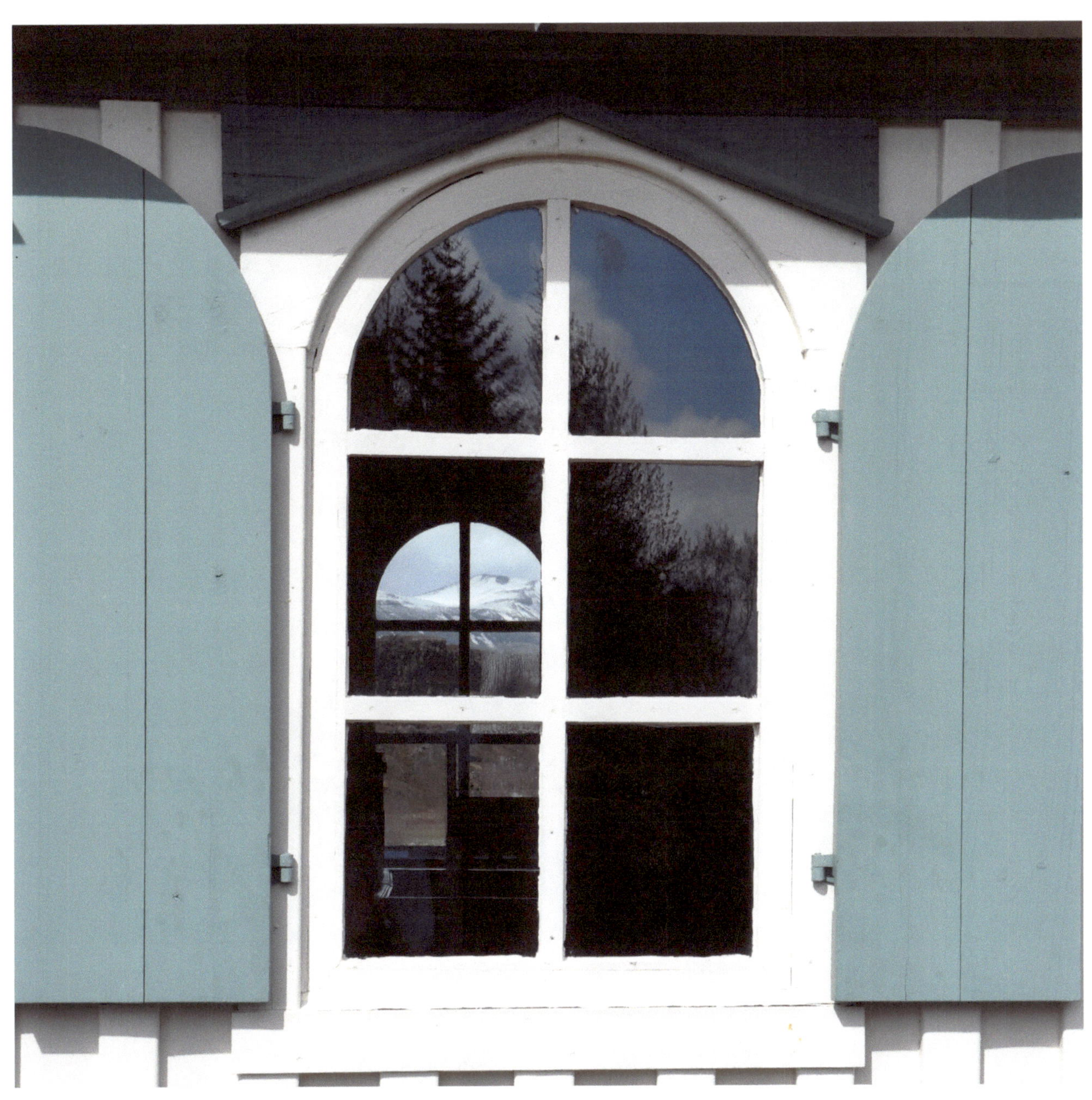

Thingvellir, Iceland

Never compare your inside with somebody else's outside.

--Hugh Macleod

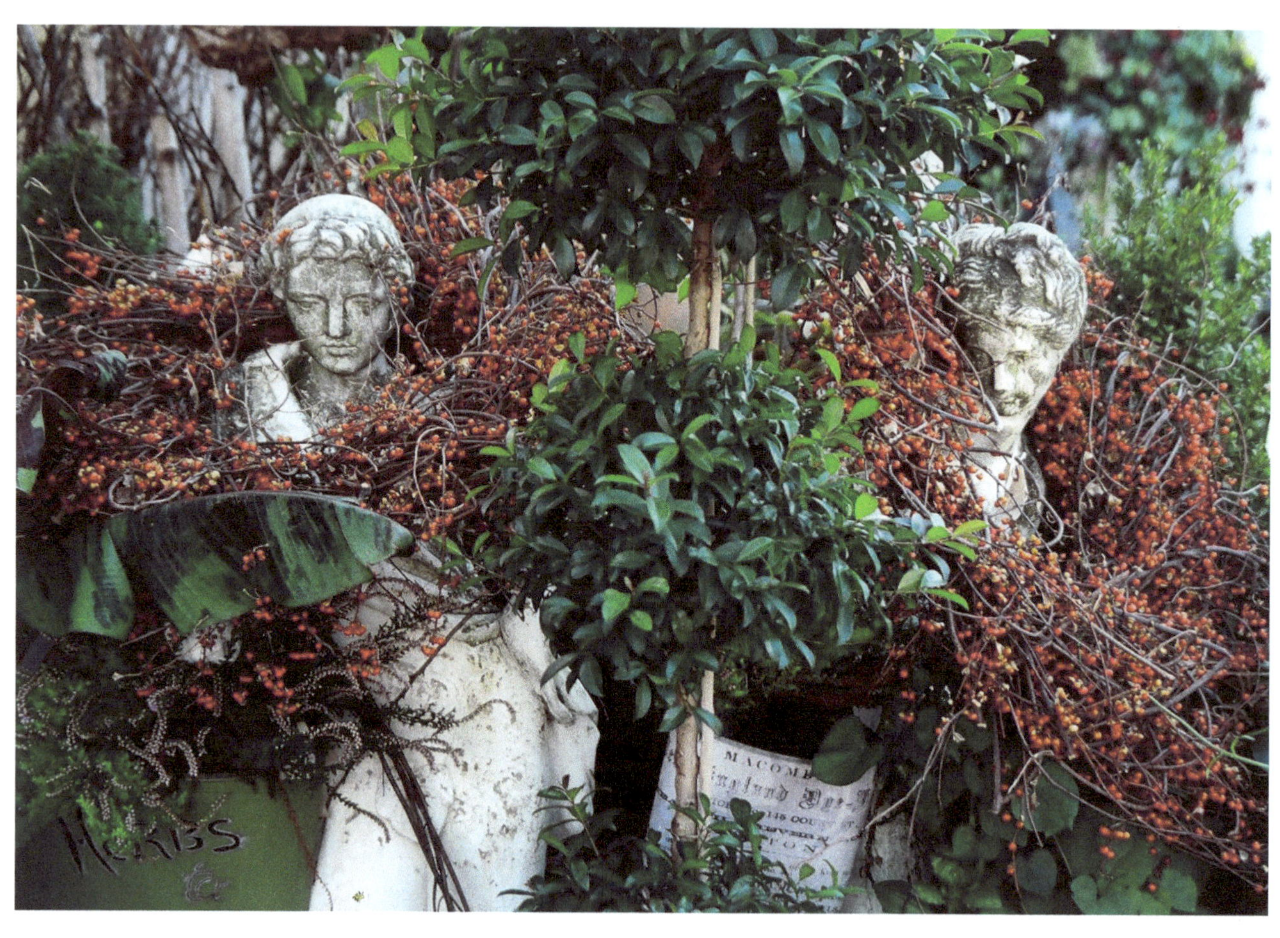

Marblehead, Massachusetts

Why should we all dress after the same fashion?
The frost never paints my windows twice alike.
--Lydia Maria Child, 1802-1880

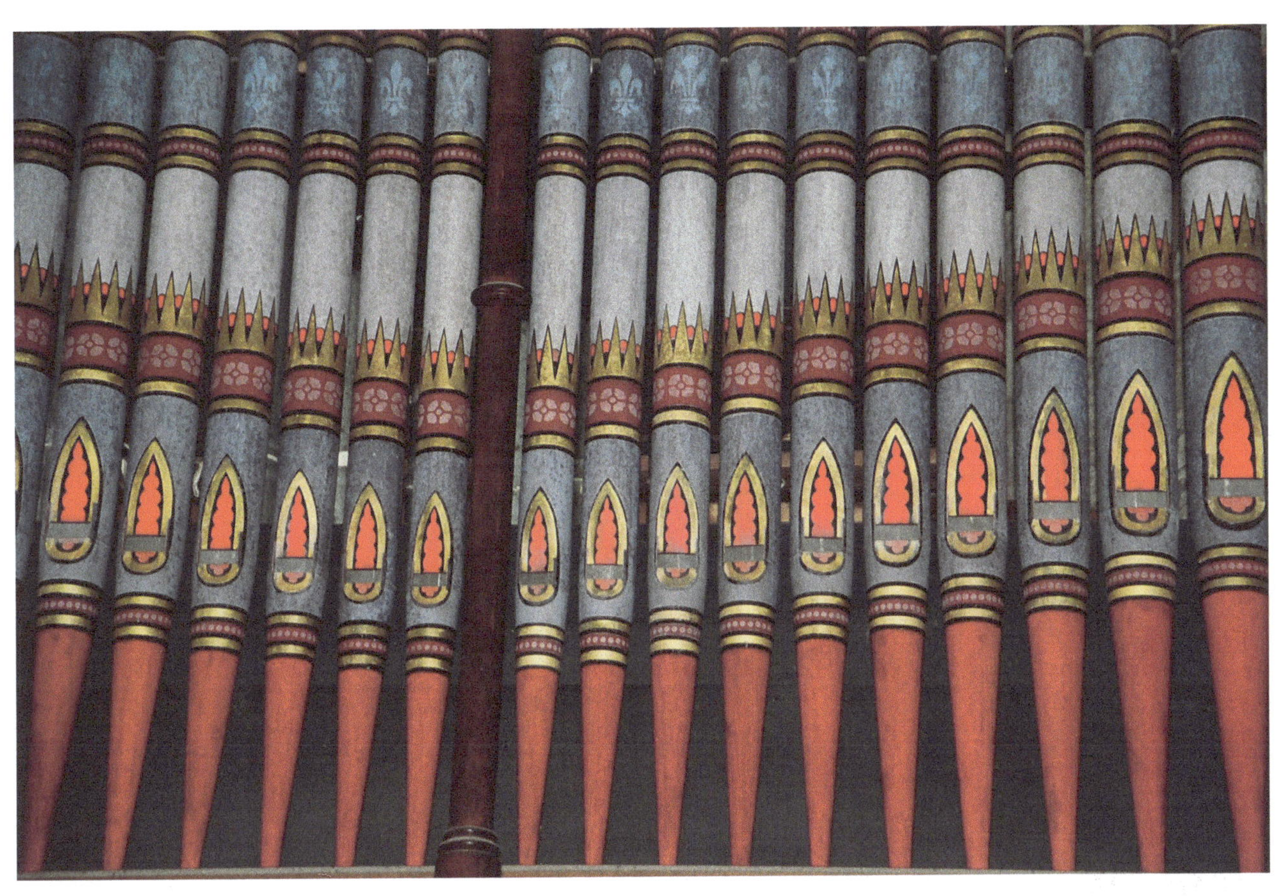

Arundel, England

You don't get harmony when everybody sings the same note.

--Doug Floyd

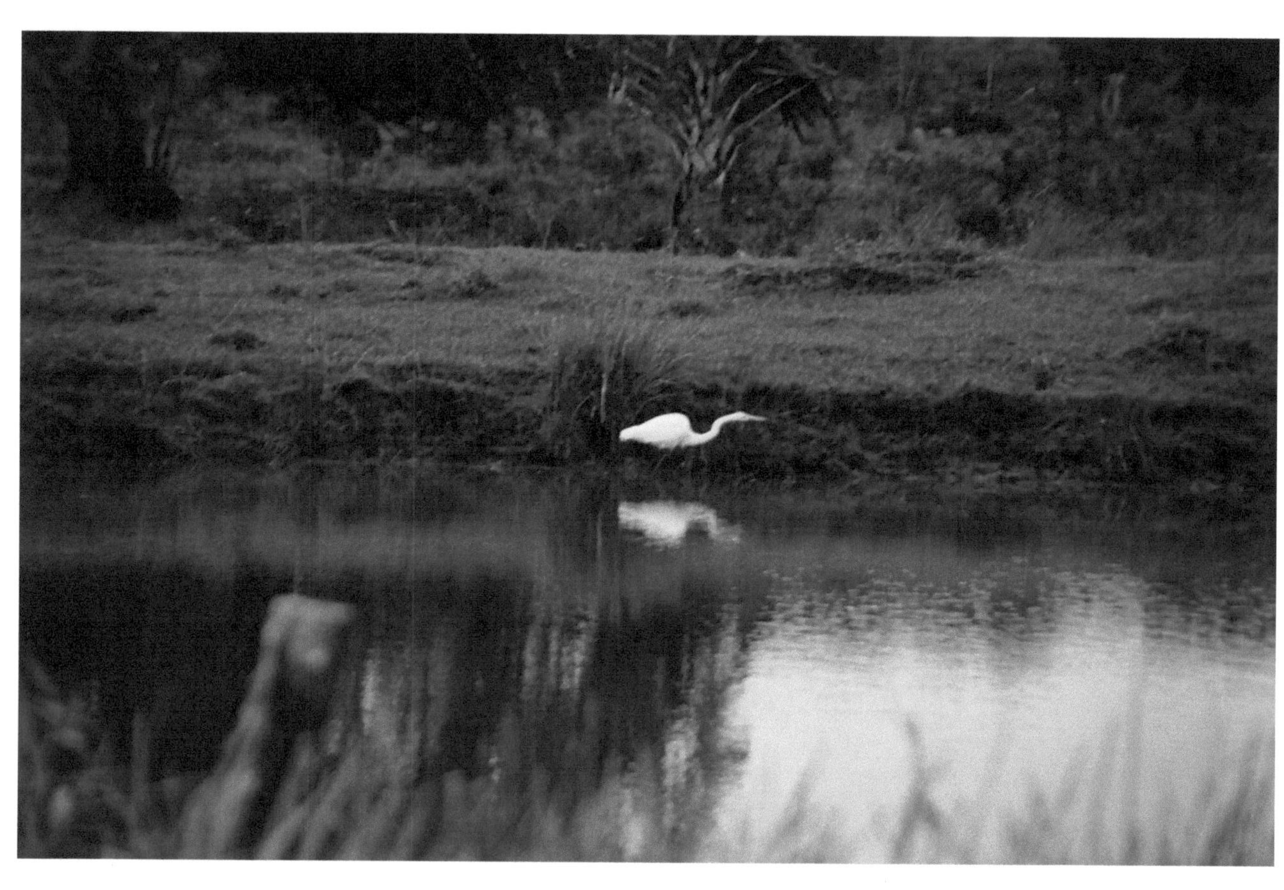

Chaa Creek, Belize

Use what talent you possess:
the woods would be very silent if no birds sang except those that sang best.
--Henry van Dyke, 1852-1933

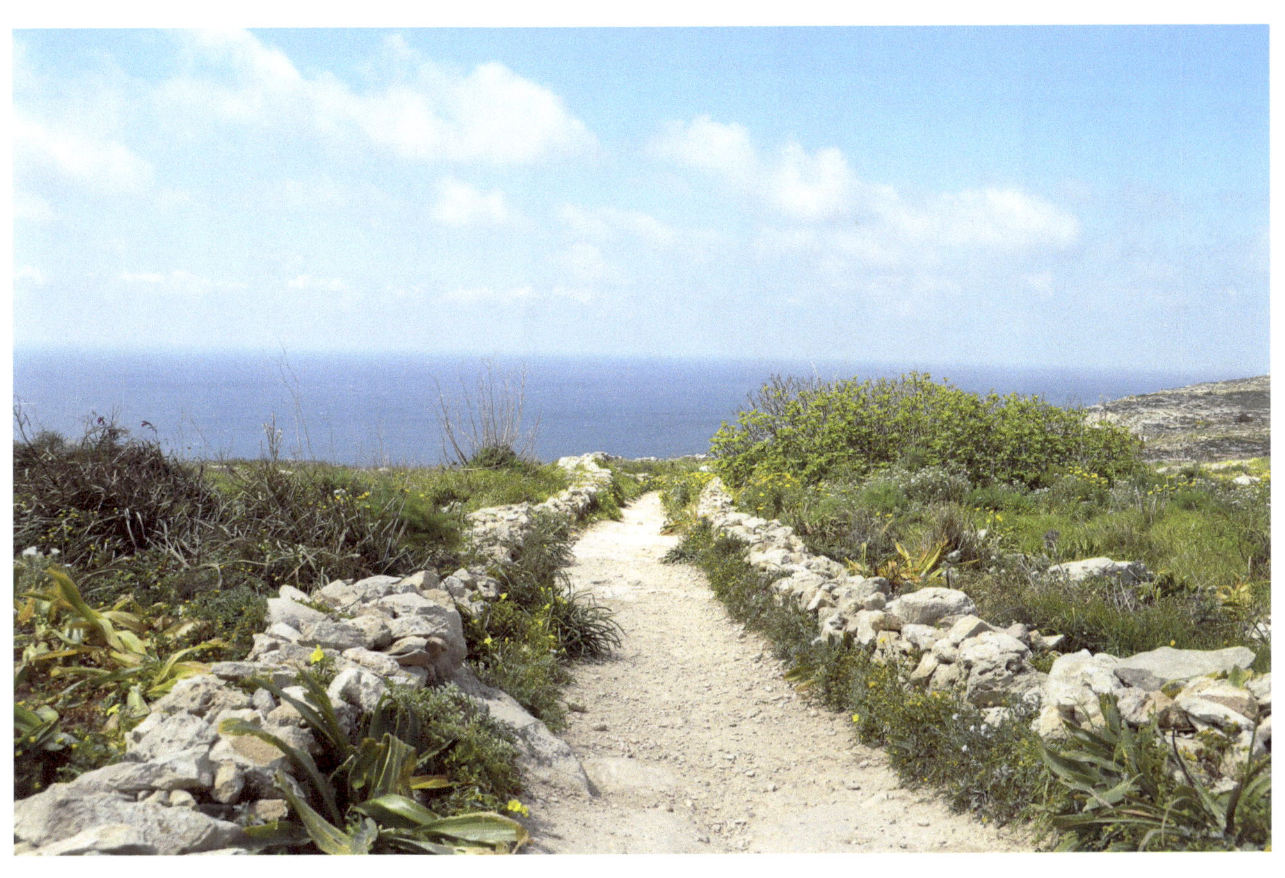

Hagar Qim, Malta

Seek out that particular mental attitude
which makes you feel most deeply and vitally alive,
along with which comes the inner voice
which says" This is the real me,"
and when you have found that attitude,
follow it.

--William James, 1842-1910

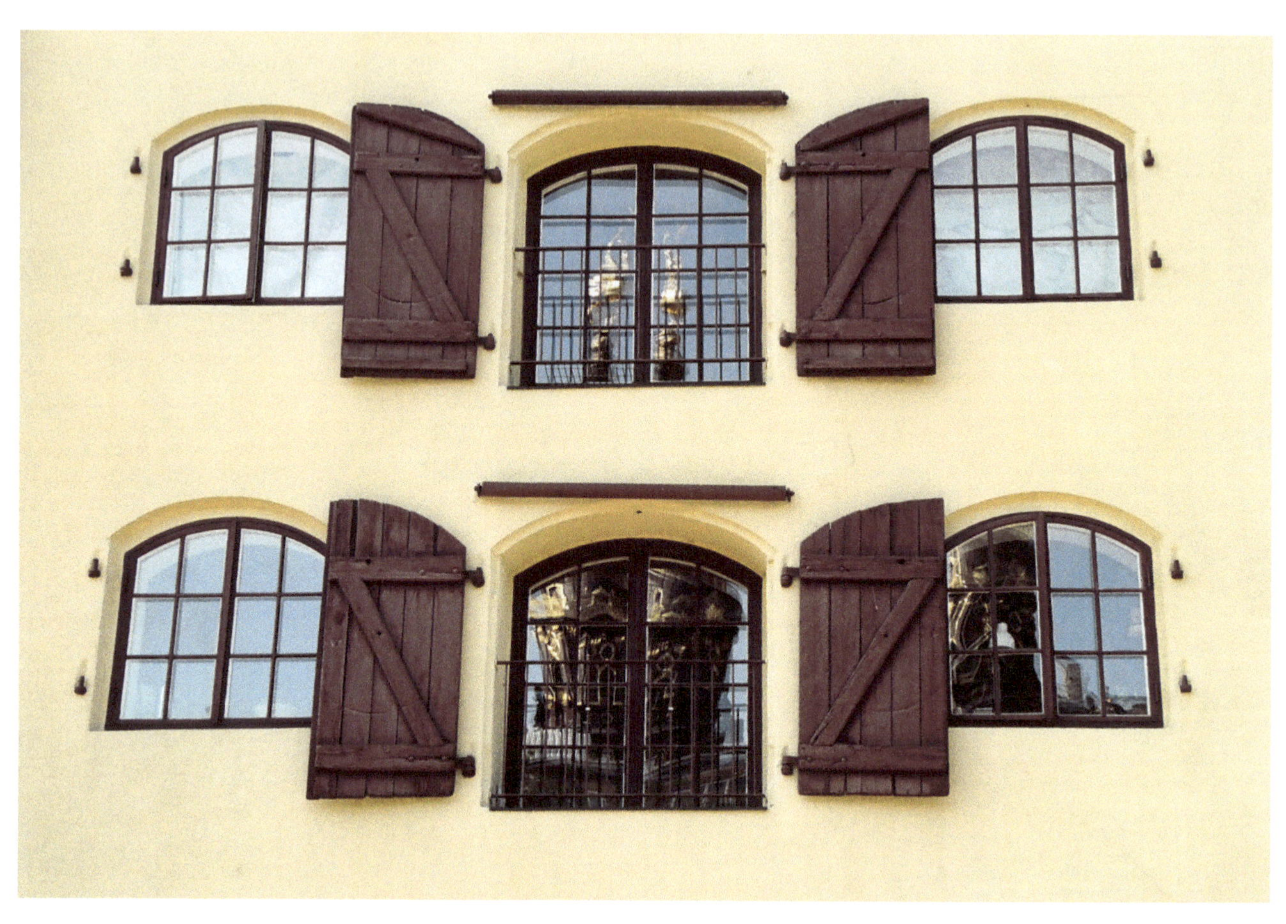

Copenhagen, Denmark

It is not easy to find happiness inside ourselves and it is impossible to find it elsewhere.

--Agnes Repplier, 1855-1950

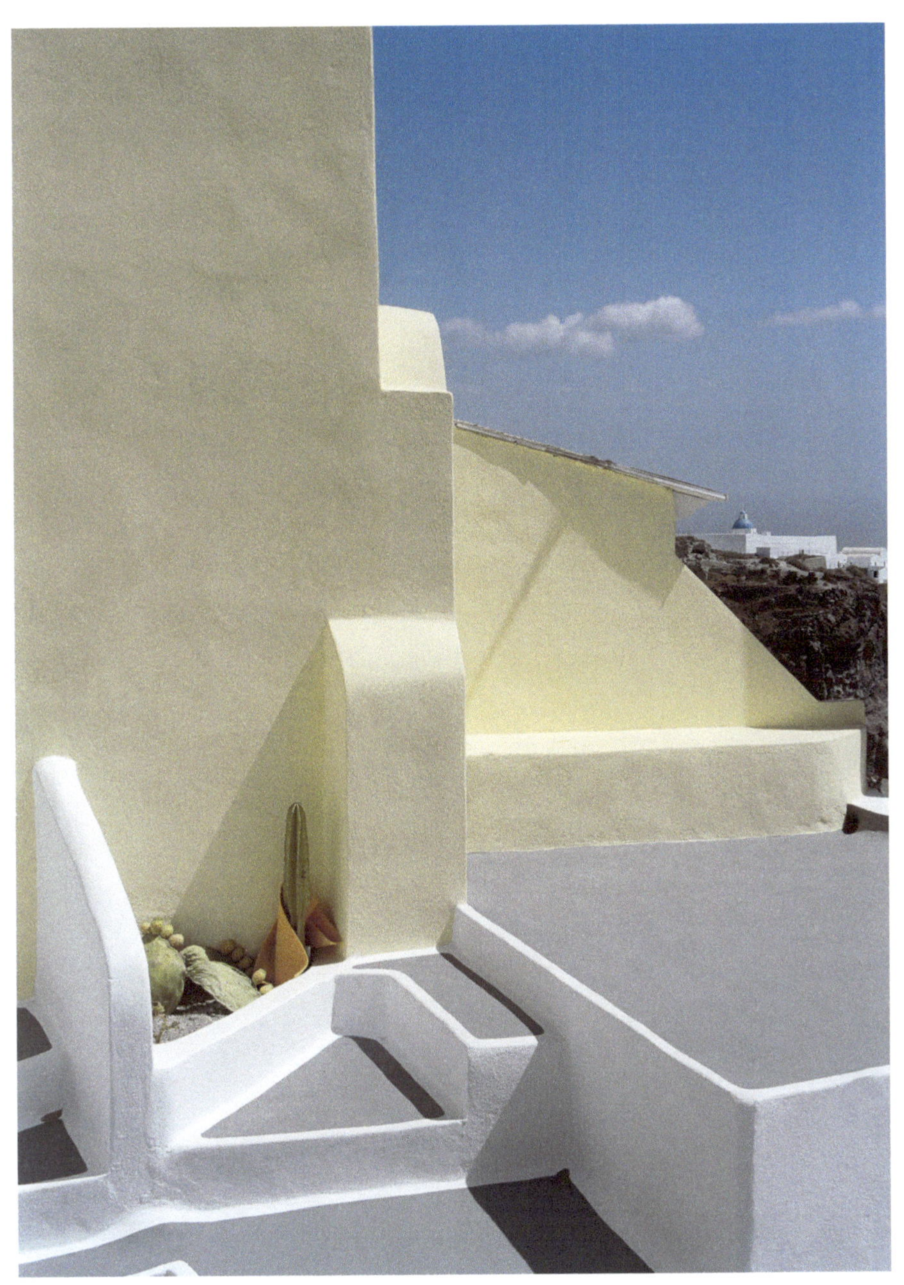

Santorini, Greece

Originality finds the unexpected but inevitable next step.

--Mason Cooley, 1927-

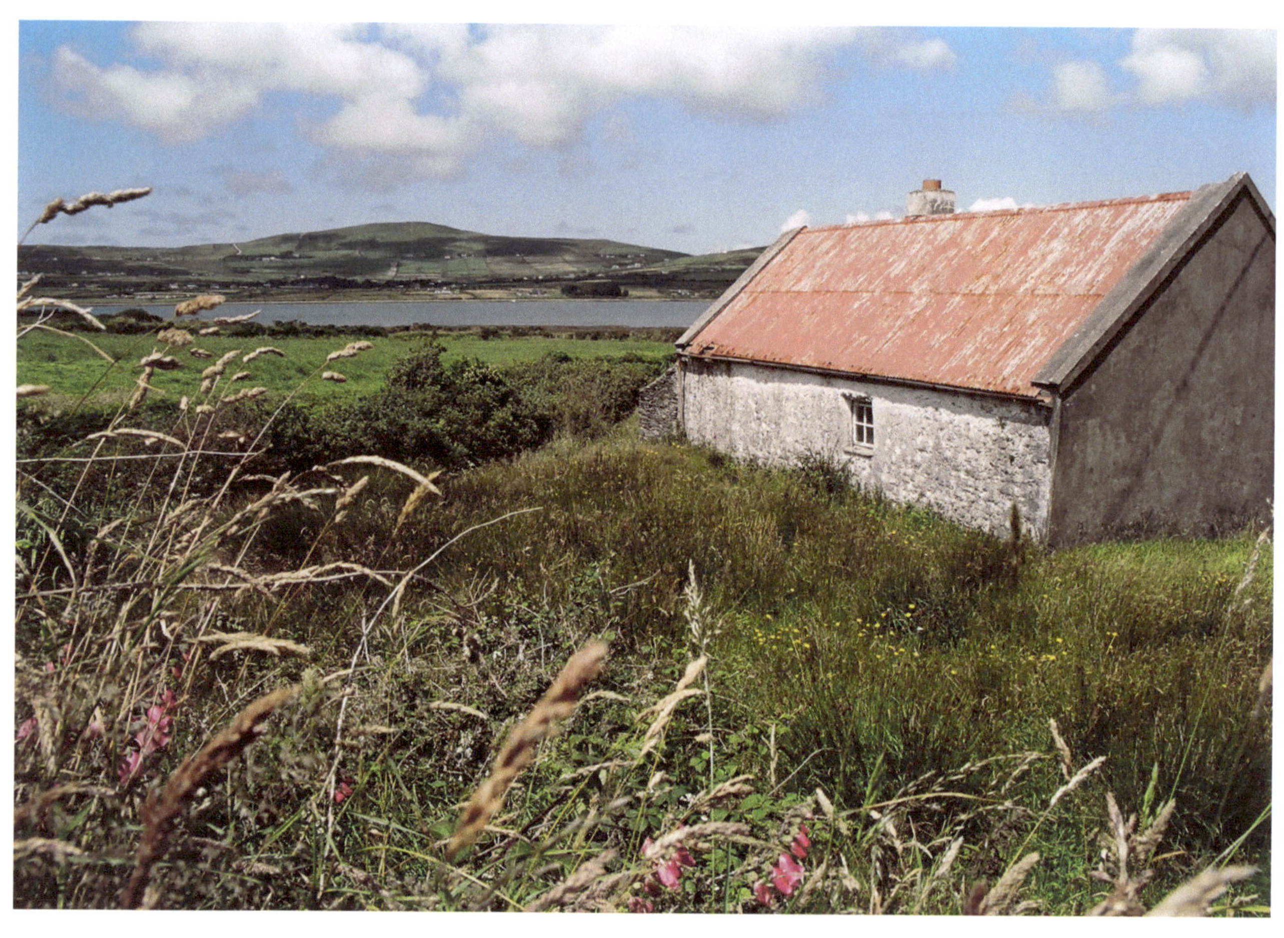

Valentia Island, Ireland

The thing that is really hard, and really amazing, is giving up on being perfect and beginning the work of becoming yourself.

--Anna Quindlen, 1953-

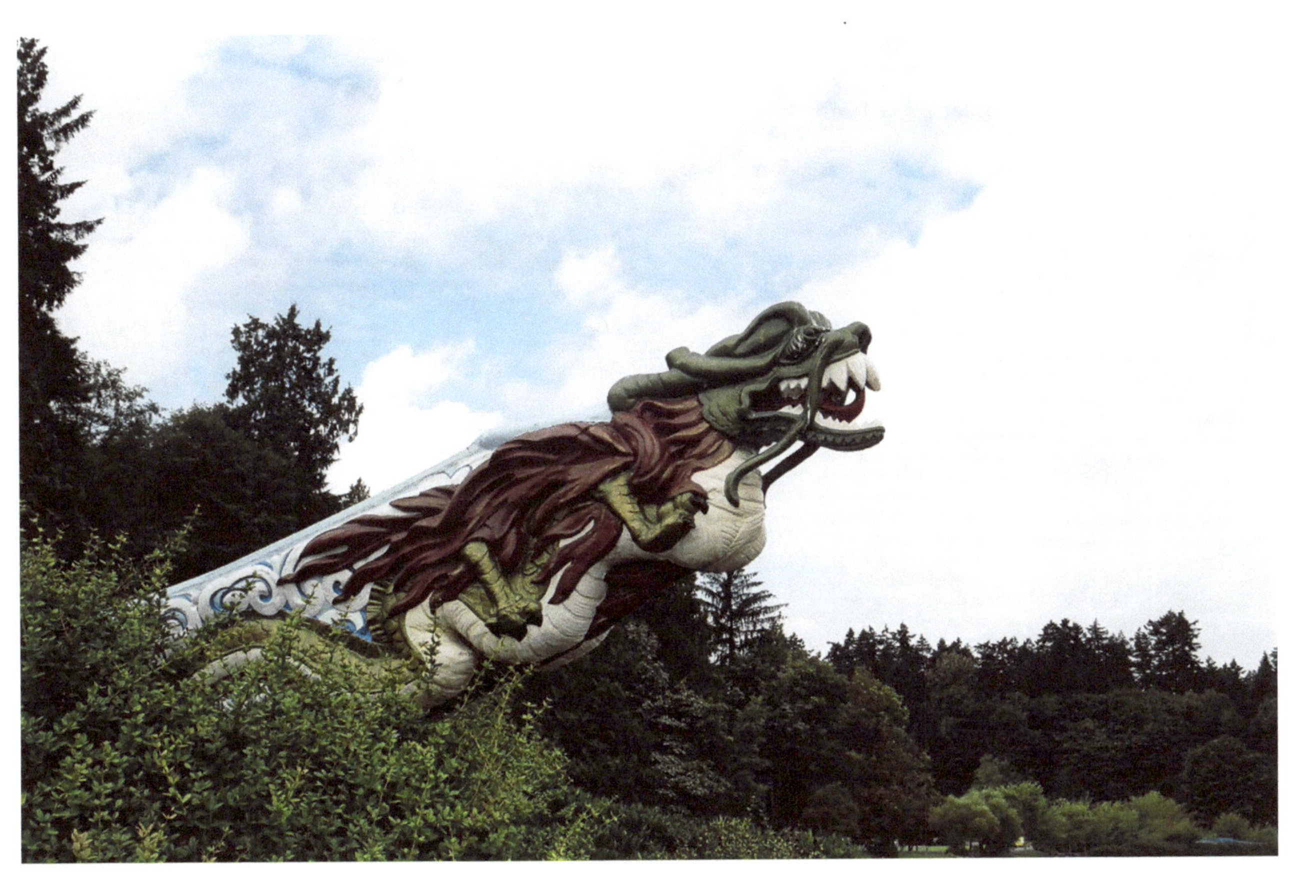

Vancouver, British Columbia

To be nobody but yourself--in a world which is doing its best to make you everybody else--
means to fight the hardest battle any human being can fight, and never stop fighting.
--e.e. cummings, 1894-1962

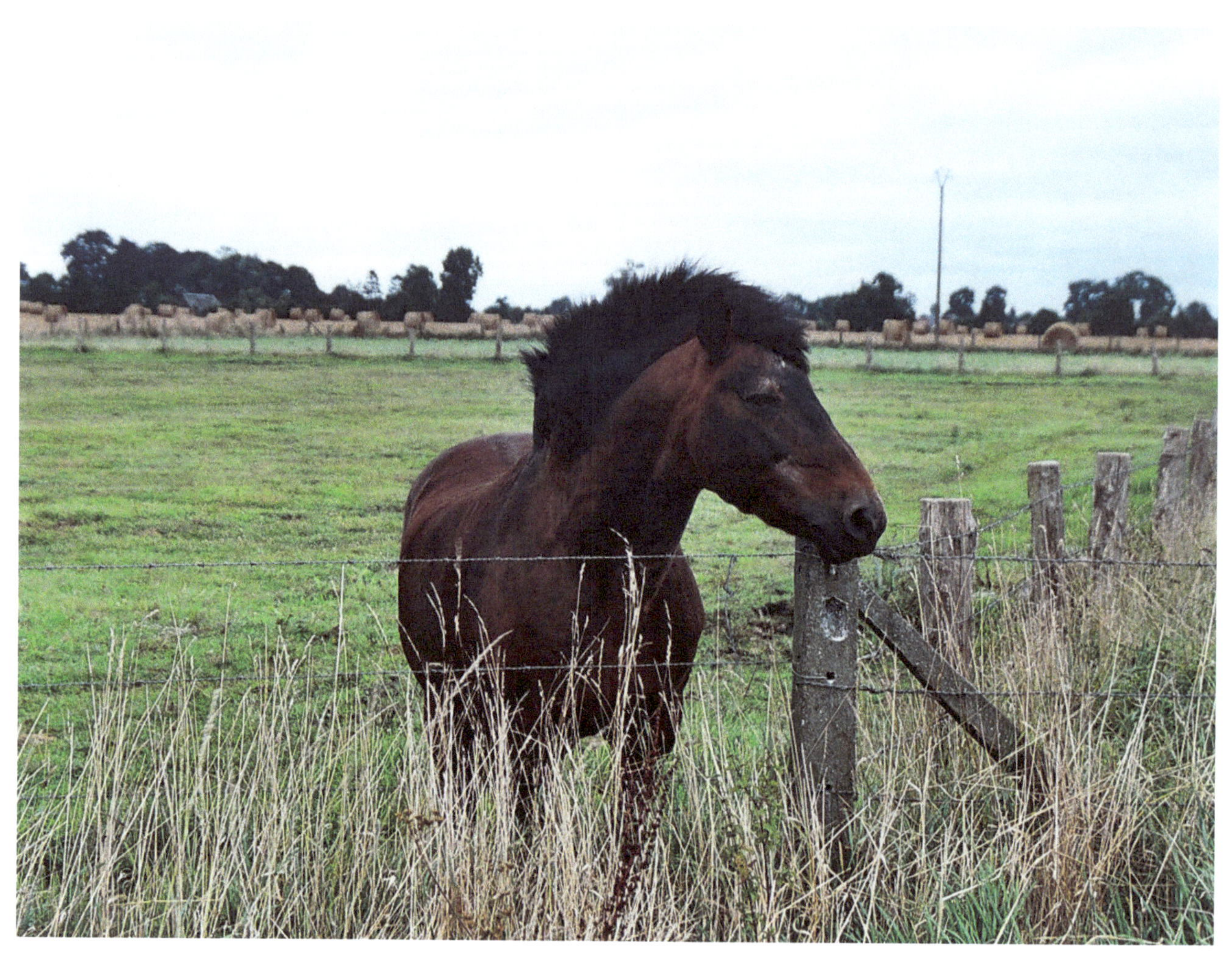

Normandy, France

With him for a sire and her for a dam, what should I be but just what I am?

--Edna St. Vincent Millay, 1892-1950

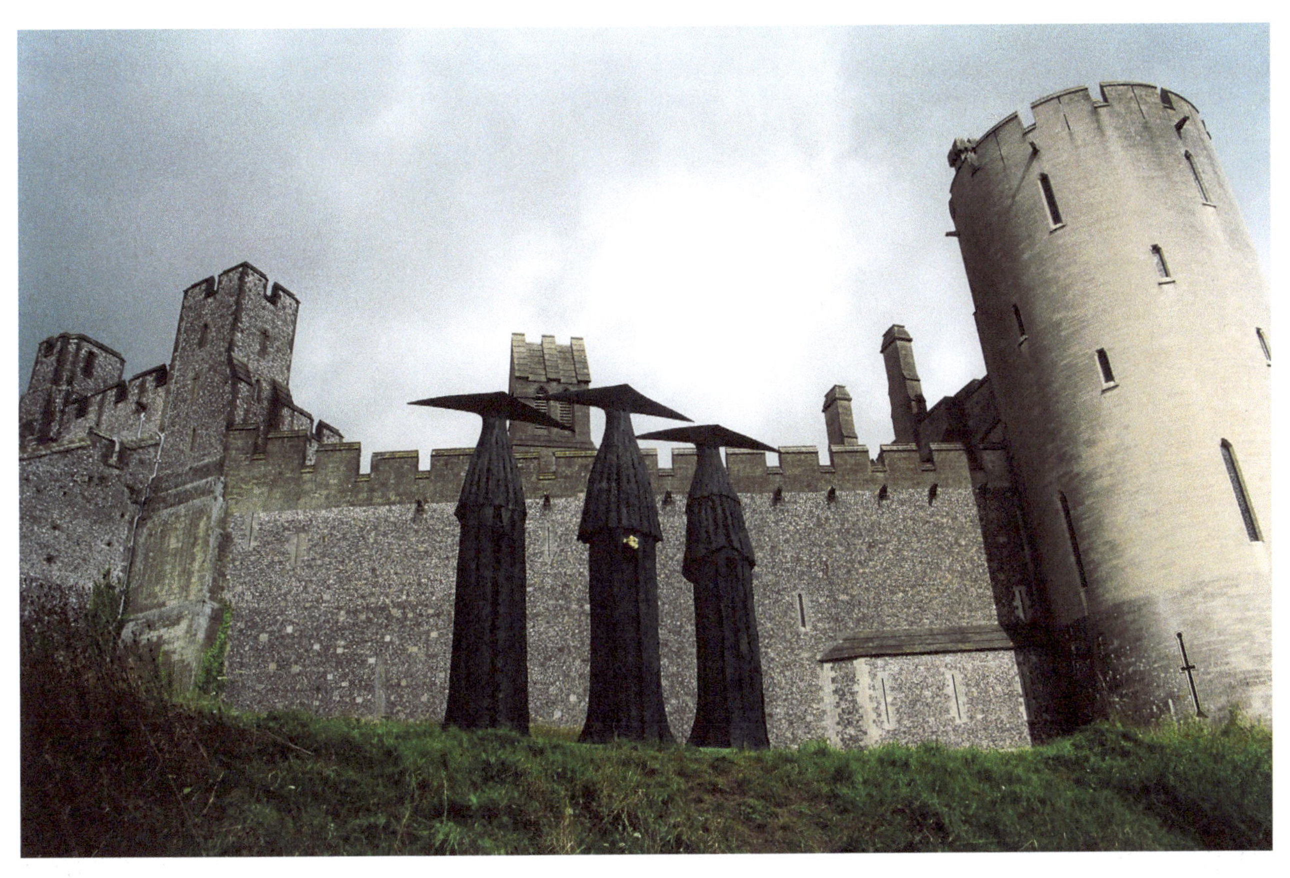

Arundel, England

Trust yourself. Think for yourself. Act for yourself. Speak for yourself. Be yourself.

Imitation is suicide.

--Marva Collins, 1936-

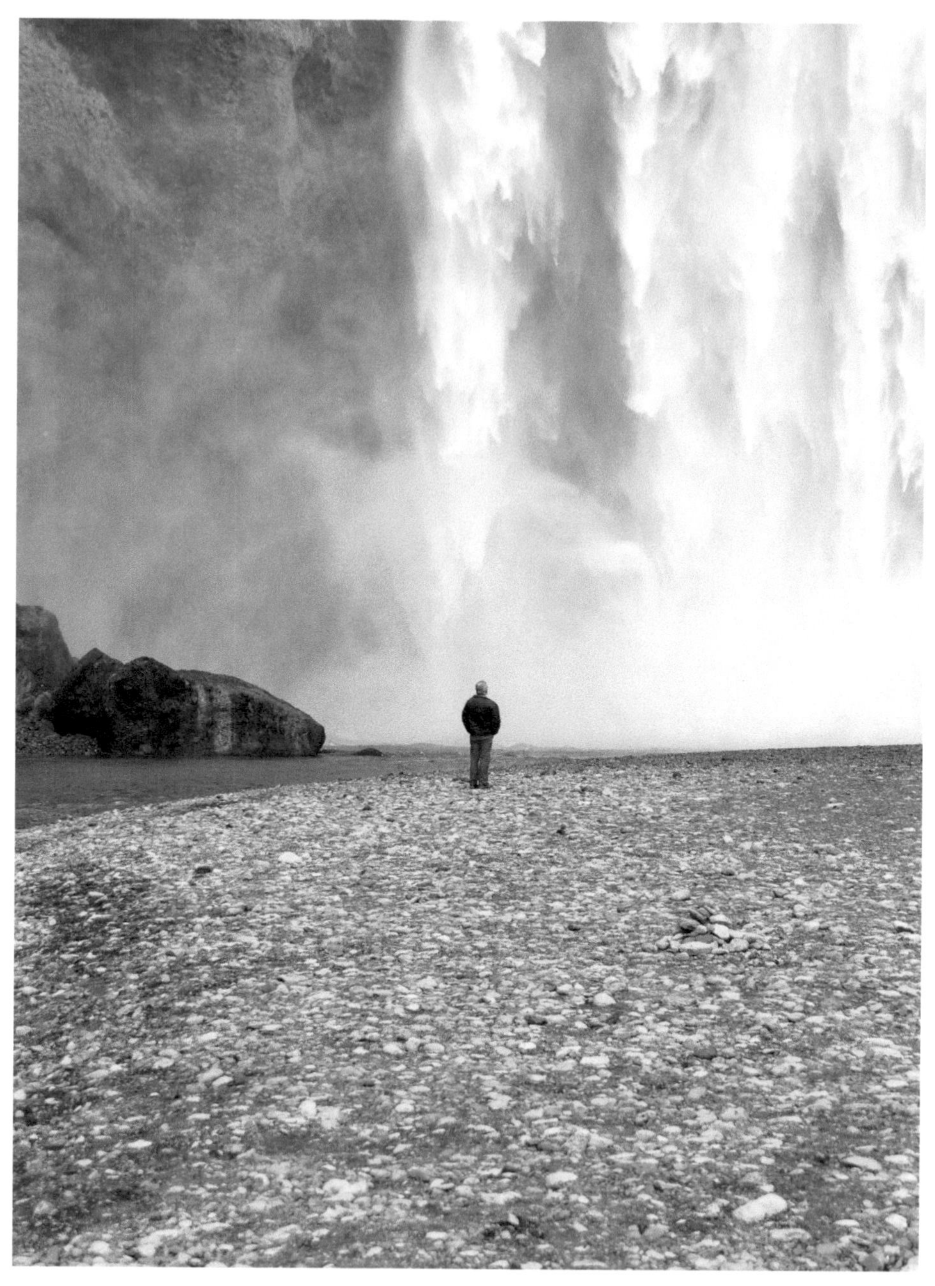

Skogafoss, Iceland

There is nothing like returning to a place that remains unchanged
to find the ways in which you yourself have altered.
--Nelson Mandela, 1918-

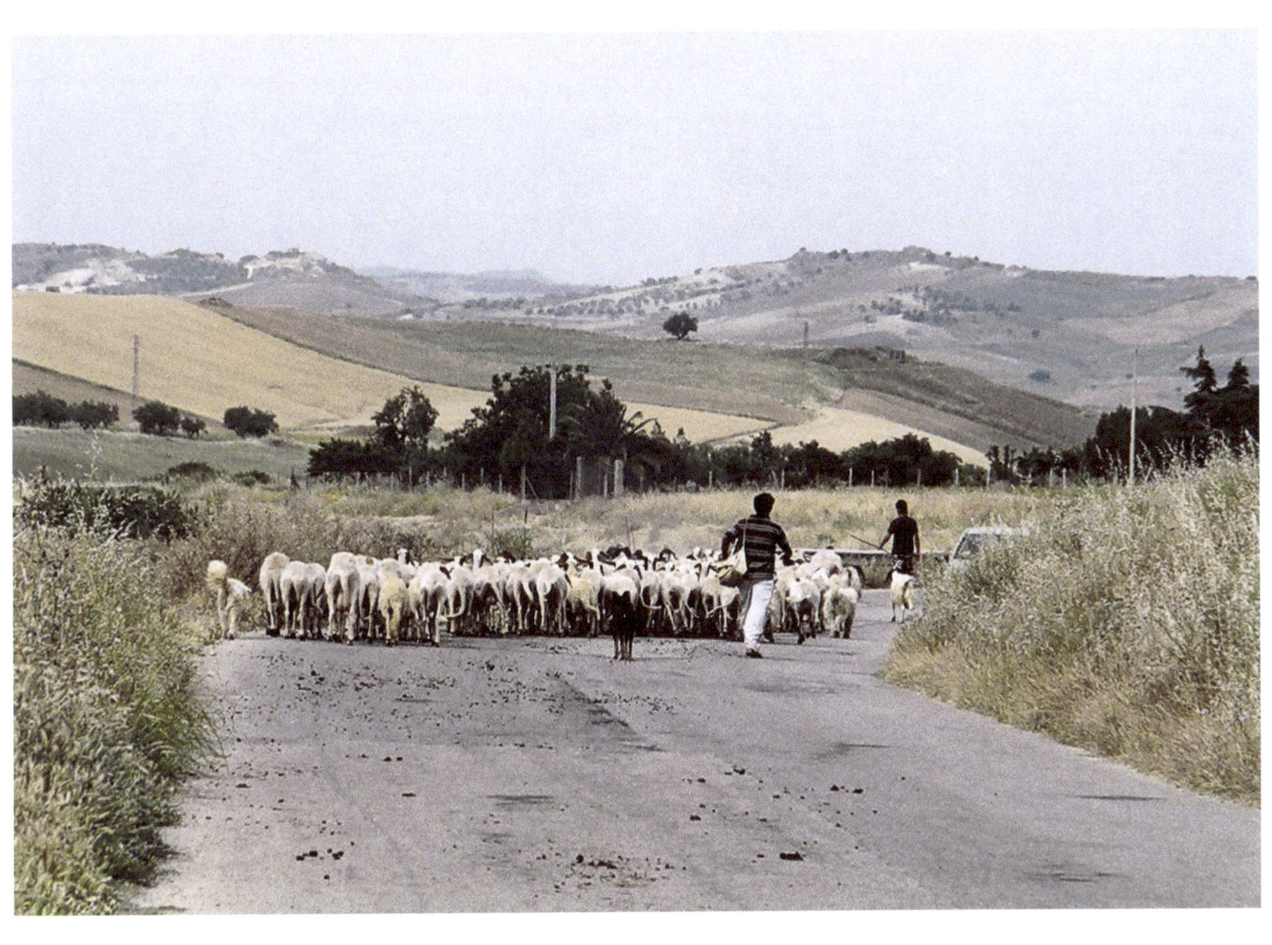

Piazza Armerina environs, Sicily

I pay no attention whatever to anybody's praise or blame.
I simply follow my own feelings.
--Wolfgang Amadeus Mozart, 1756-1791

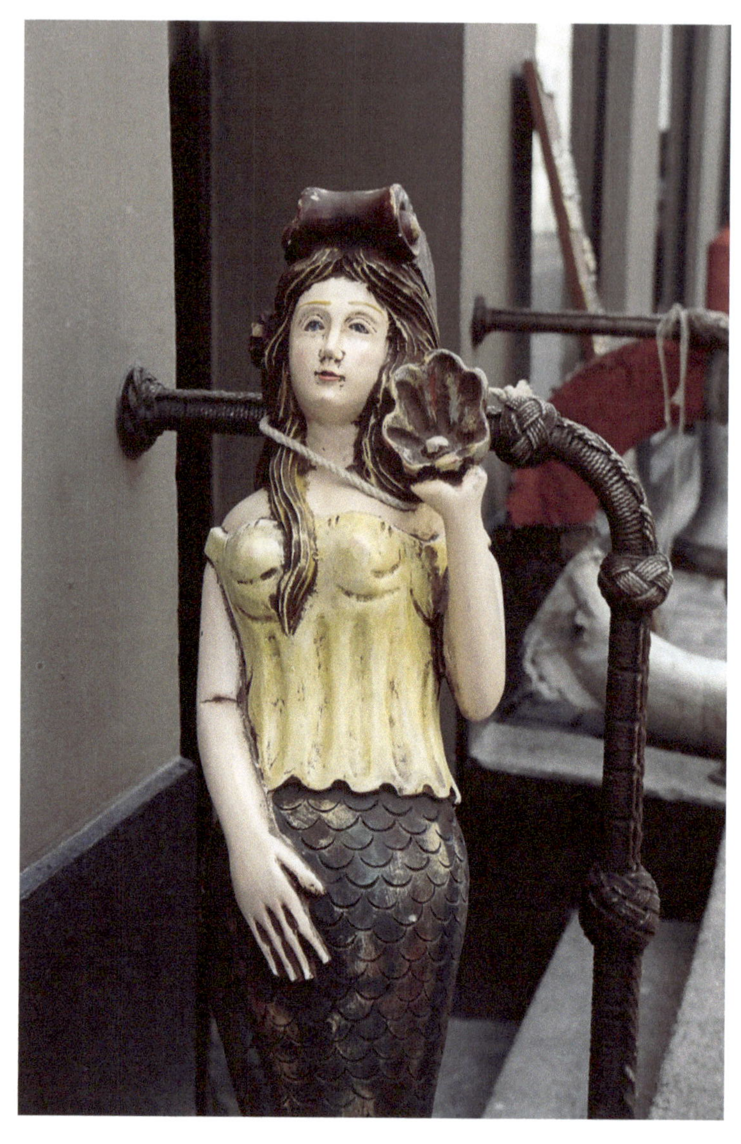

Copenhagen, Denmark

In the very struggle to be like someone else
rather than be one's own true self,
or to do one's best in one's own environment,
a child is in danger of losing the pearl that is usually beyond price--
the integrity of his (or her) own soul.
--Sophia Lyon Fahs, 1876-1978

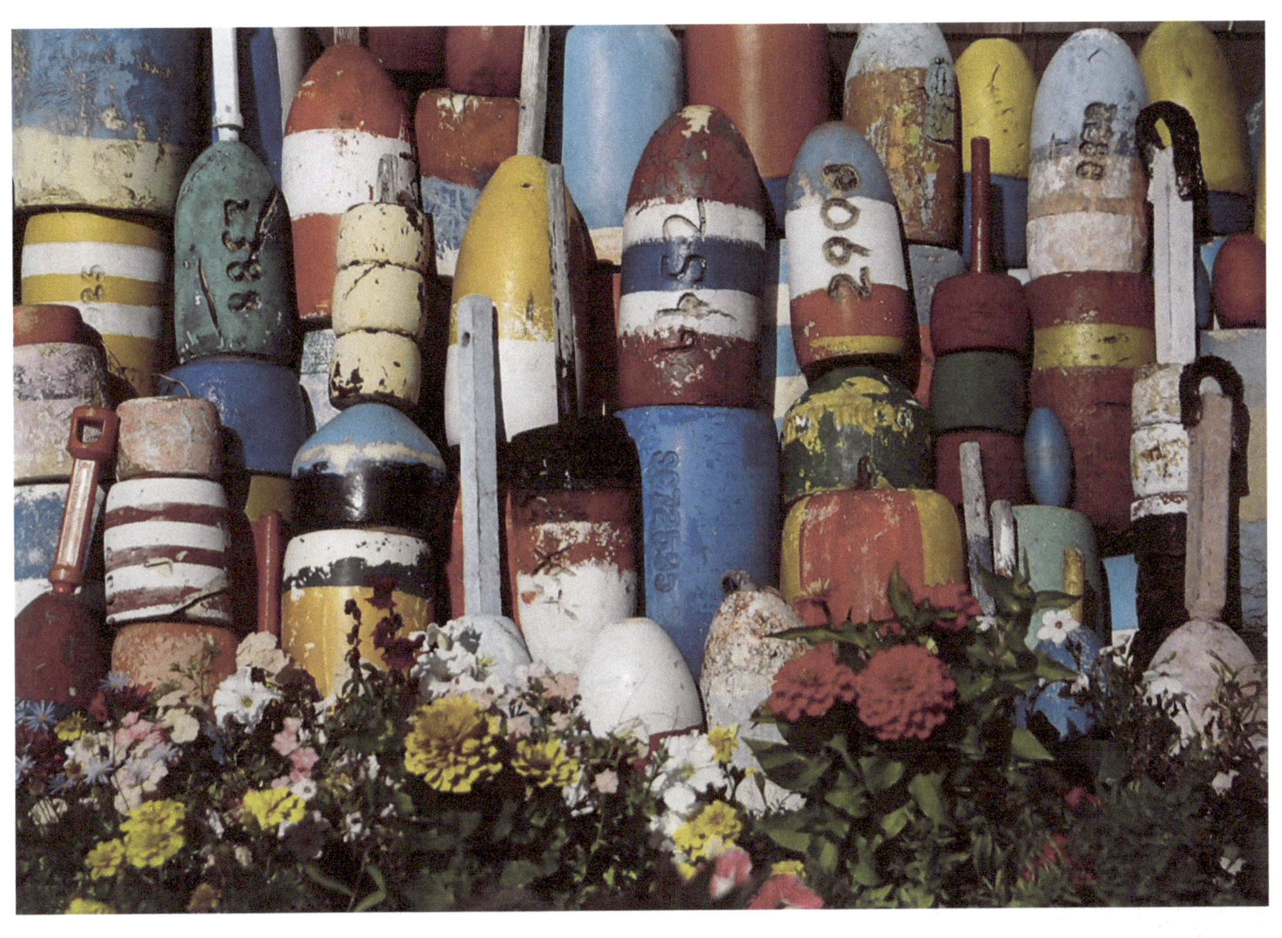

Rockport, Massachusetts

If I try to be like him, who will be like me?

--Yiddish proverb

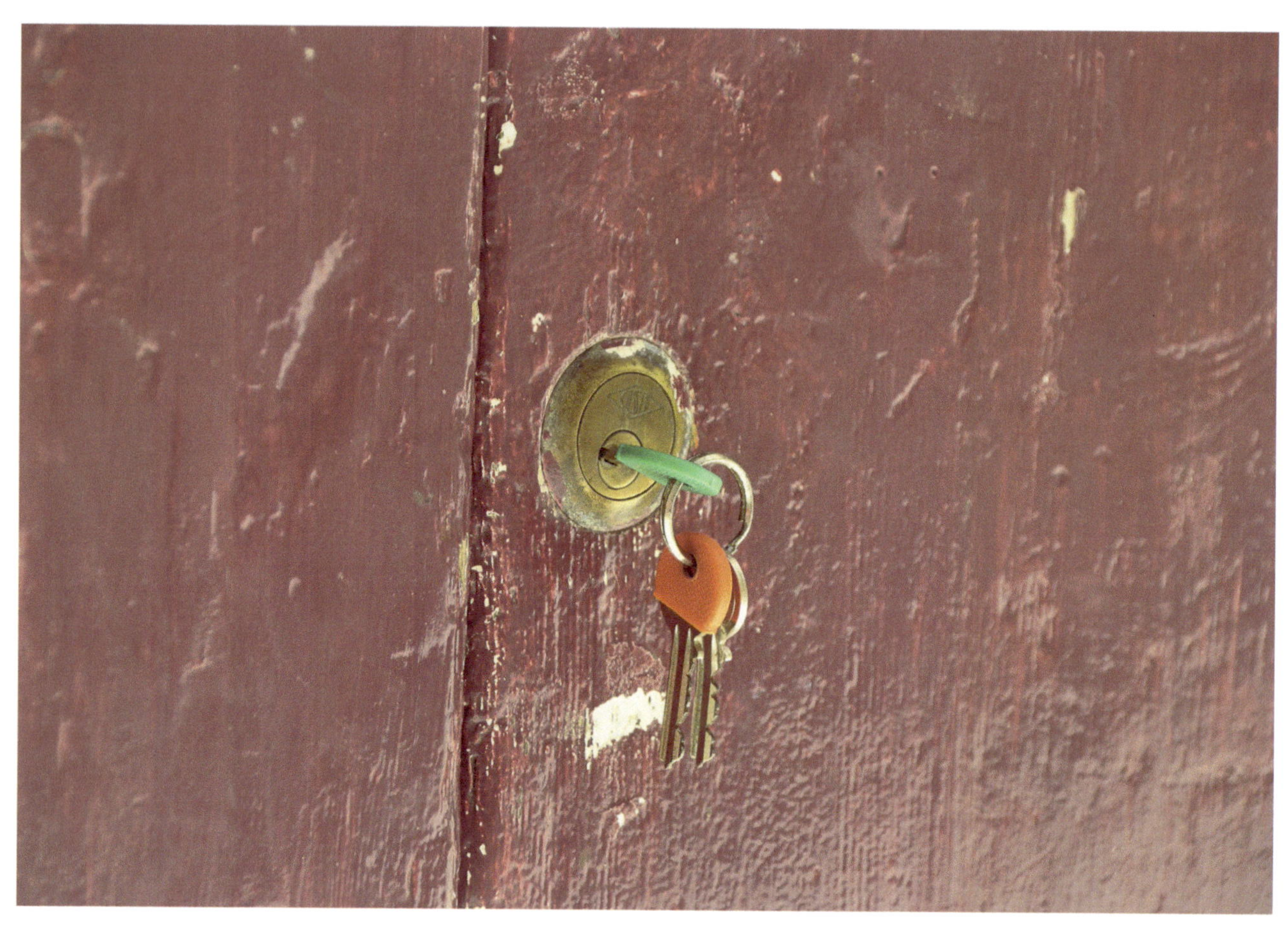

Gozo, Malta

In oneself lies the whole world and if you know how to look and learn,
the door is there and the key is in your hand.
Nobody on earth can give you either the key or the door to open,
except yourself.
--Krishnamarti

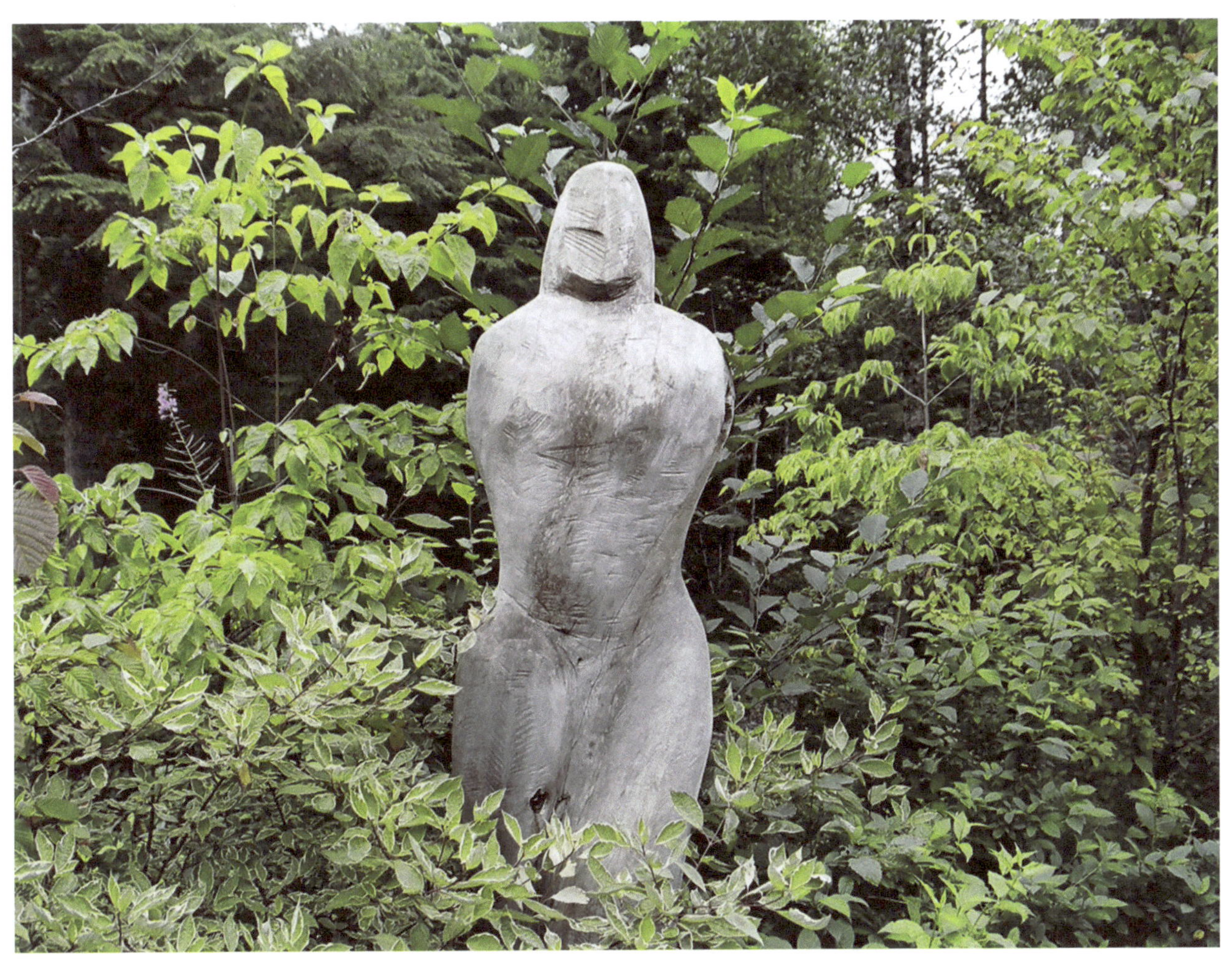

Tofino Botanical Gardens, British Columbia

I am as my creator made me
and since he is satisfied, so am I.
--Minnie Smith, 1940-

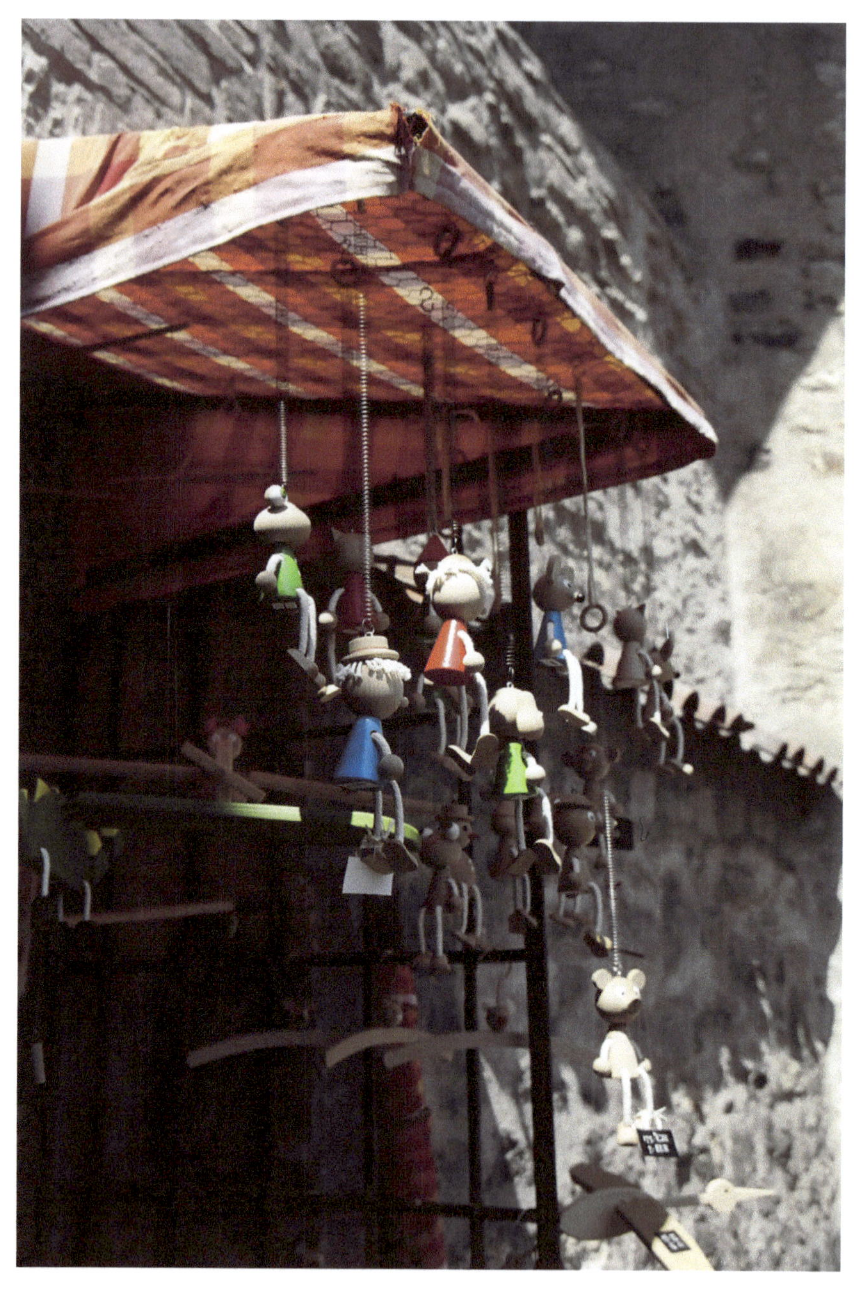

Prague, Czech Republic

Let me listen to me and not to them.

--Gertrude Stein, 1874-1946

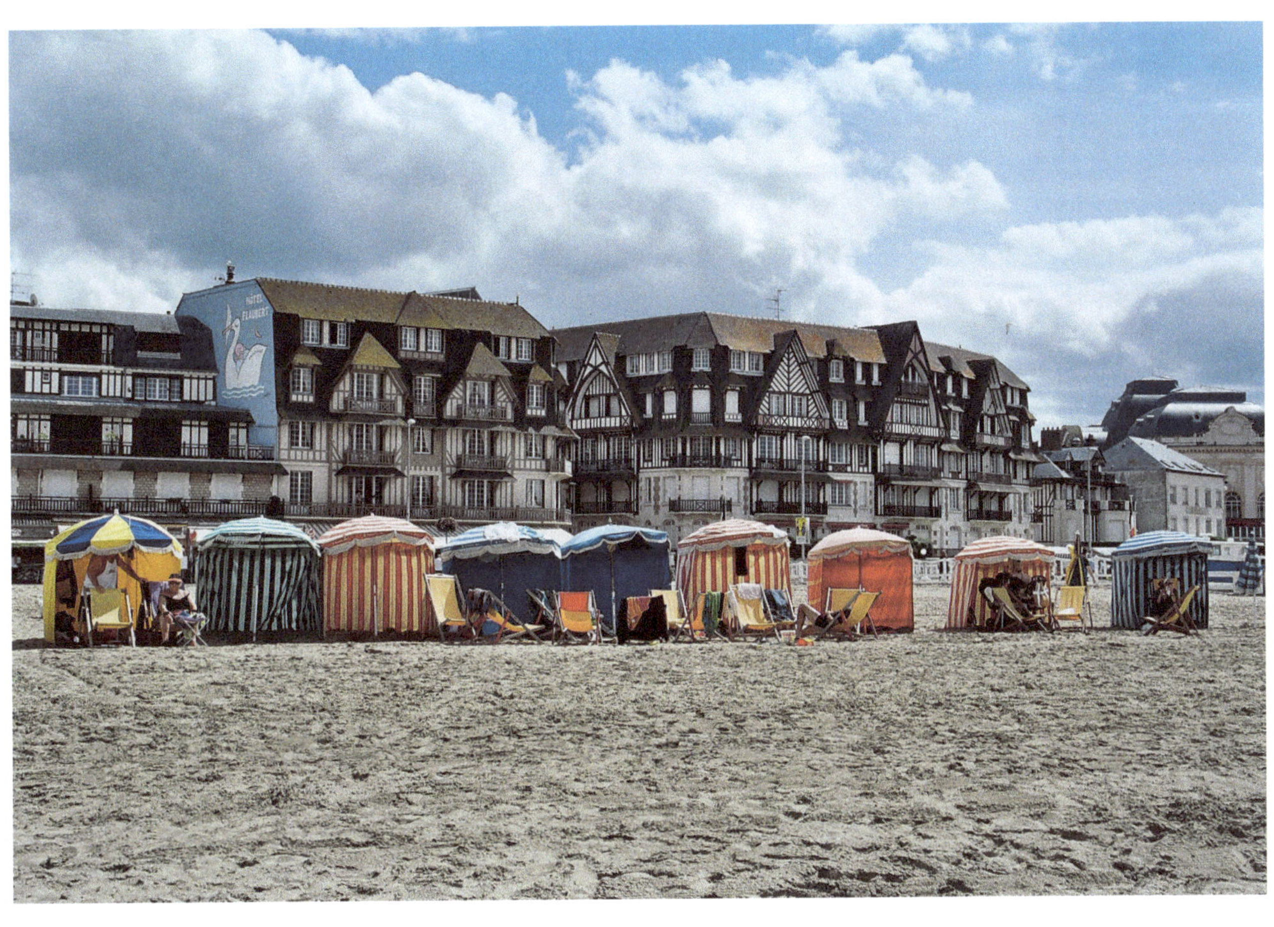

Trouville, France

If you ask me what I came into this world to do, I will tell you;

I came to live out loud.

--Emile Zola, 1840-1902

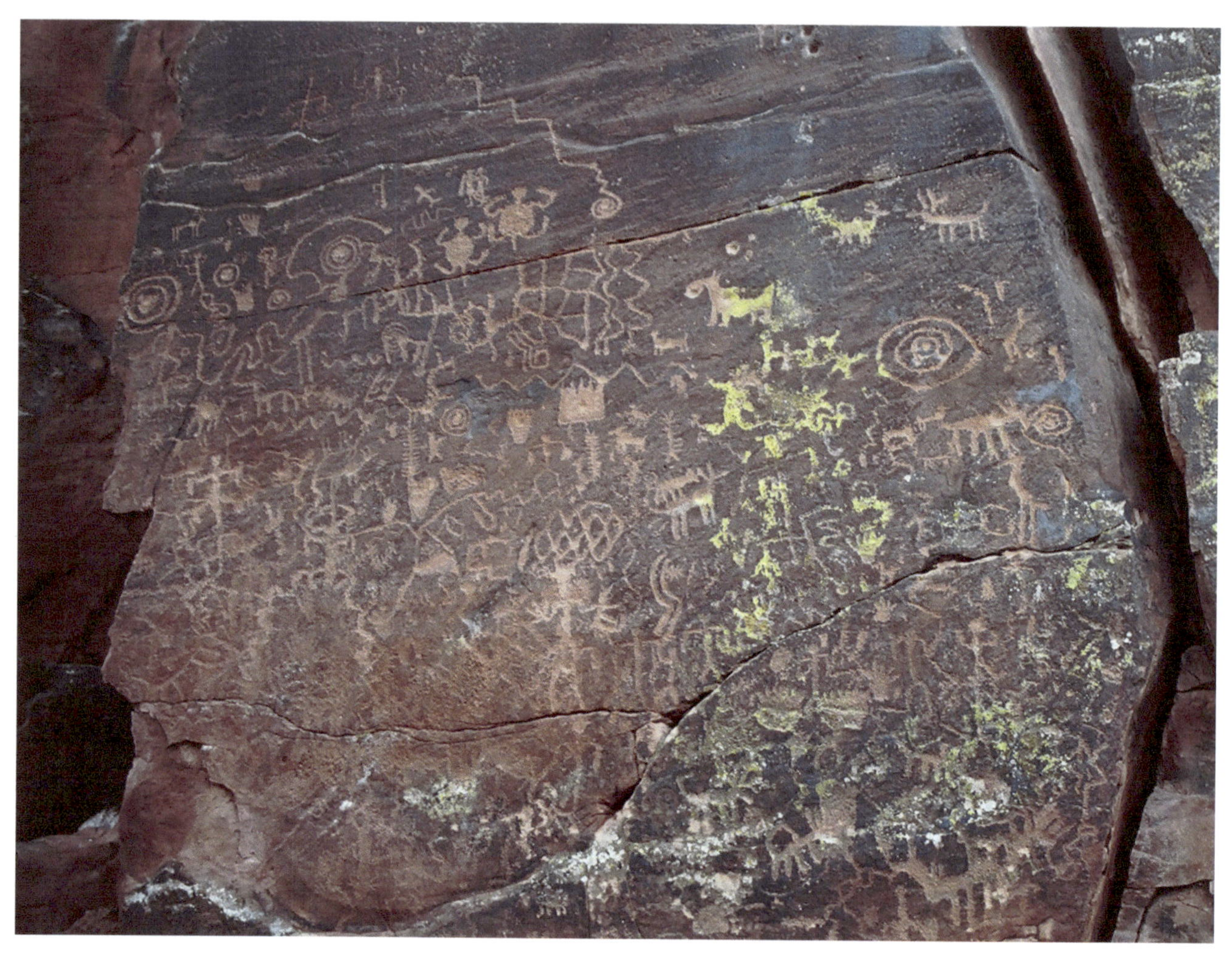

V-Bar-V Heritage Site, Arizona

You have brains in your head, You have feet in your shoes, You can steer yourself
In any direction you choose.
--Dr. Seuss, 1904-1991

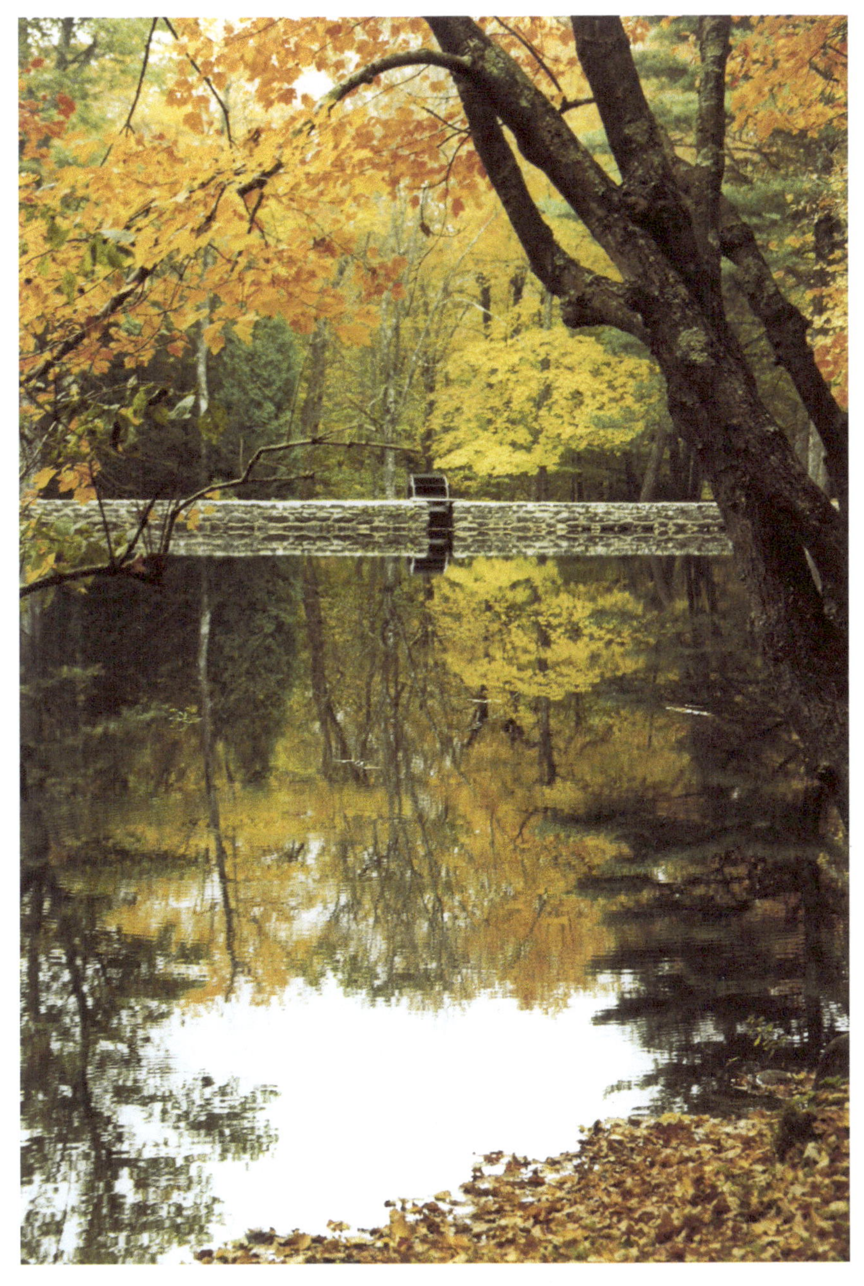

Chatfield Hollow, Connecticut

There is an art of which every man should be a master, the art of reflection.
If you are not a thinking man, to what purpose are you a man at all?
--William Hart Coleridge, 1789-1842

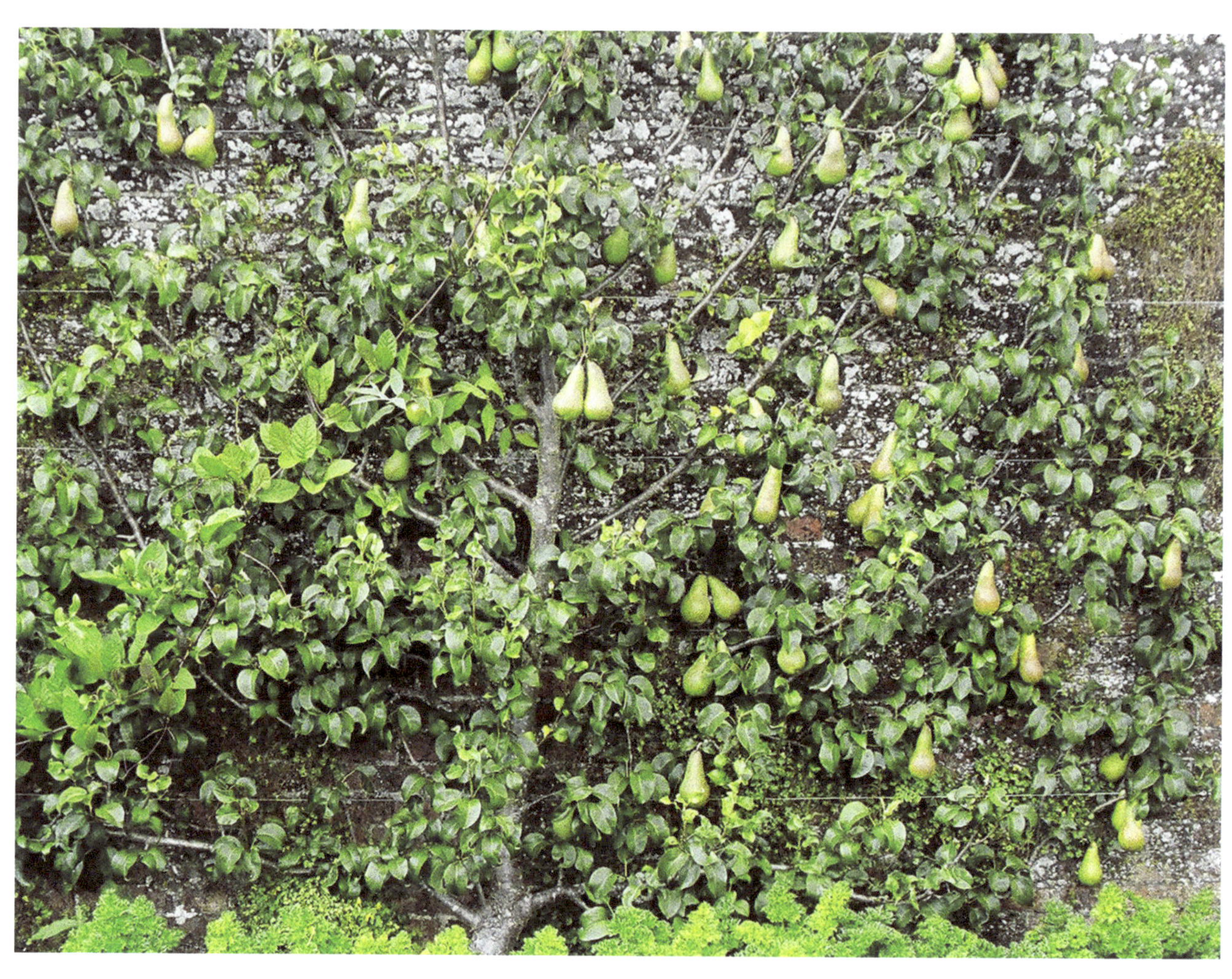

Arundel, England

If you stand up and be counted,
from time to time you may get yourself knocked down...
A man flattened by an opponent can get up again.
A man flattened by conformity stays down for good.
---Thomas J. Watson, 1874-1956

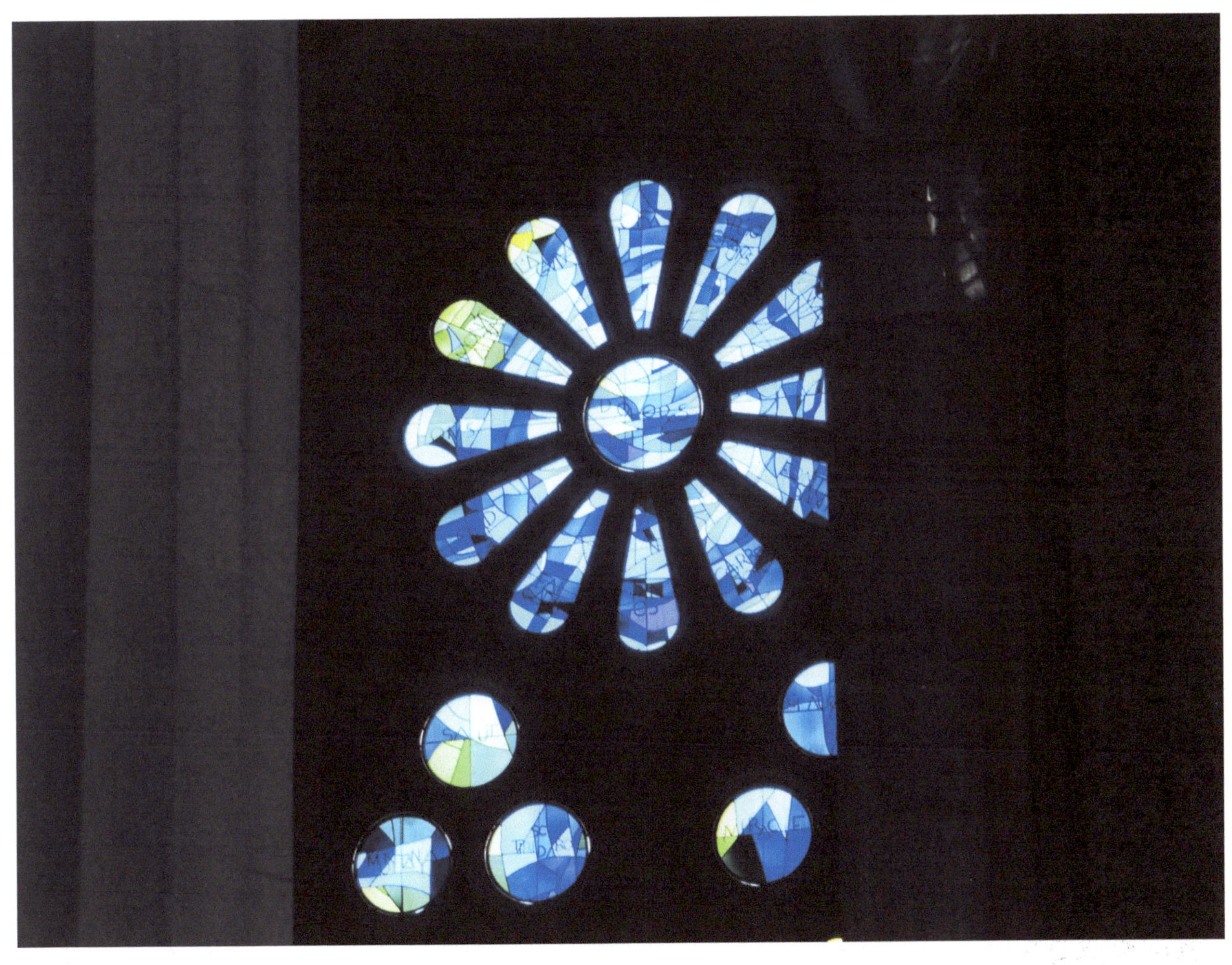

Barcelona, Spain

Your integrity is your destiny--
It is the light that guides our way.
--Heraclitus, 535-475 B.C.

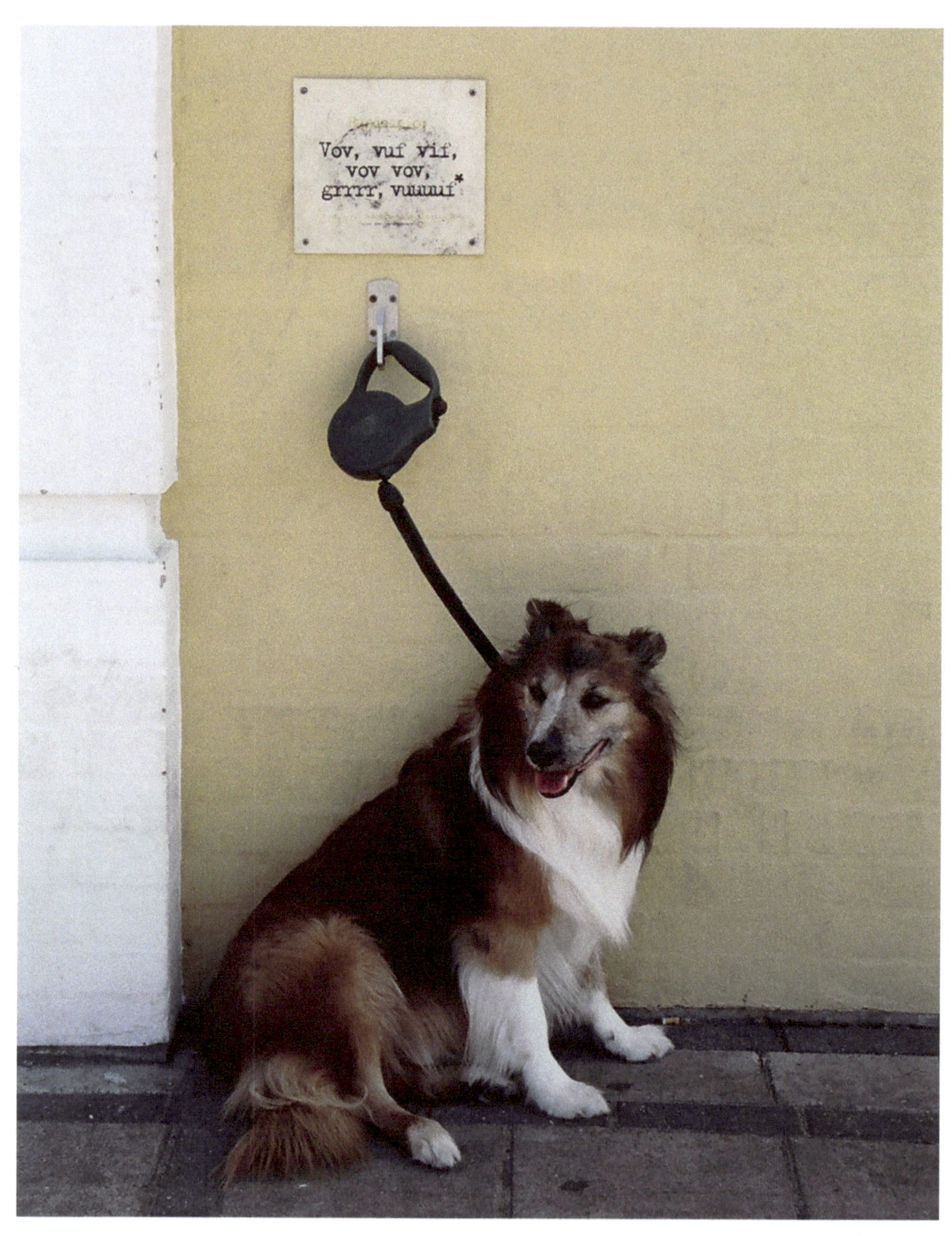

Skagen, Denmark

If we value the pursuit of knowledge,
we must be free to follow wherever that search may lead us.
The free mind is not a barking dog, to be tethered on a ten-foot chain.
--Adlai E. Stevenson, Jr., 1900-1965

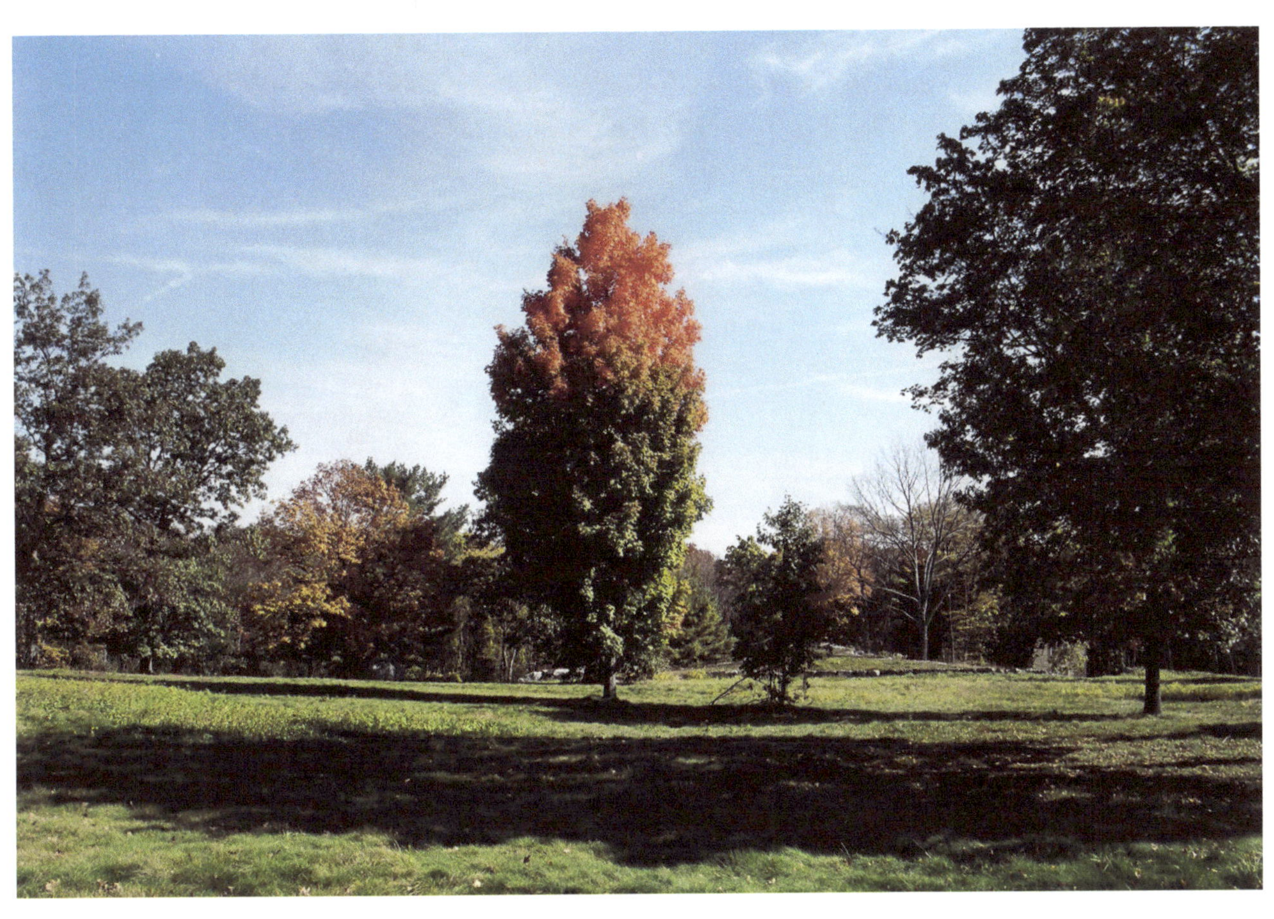

Concord, Massachusetts

When we are no longer able to change a situation...

we are challenged to change ourselves.

--Viktor Frankl, 1905-1997

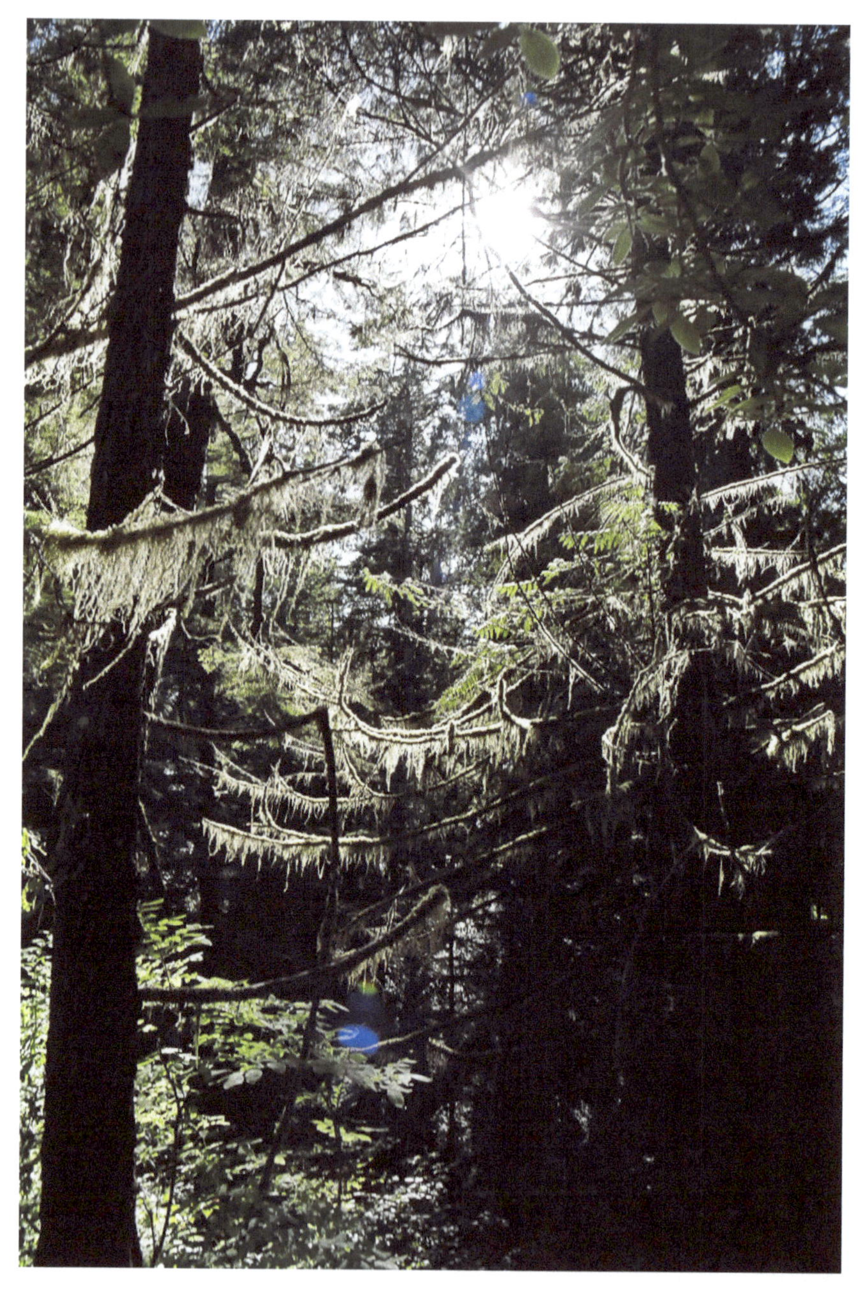

Cathedral Forest, British Columbia

The moment we begin to fear the opinions of others and hesitate to tell the truth that is in us...the divine floods of light and life no longer flow into our souls.

--Elizabeth Cady Stanton, 1815-1902

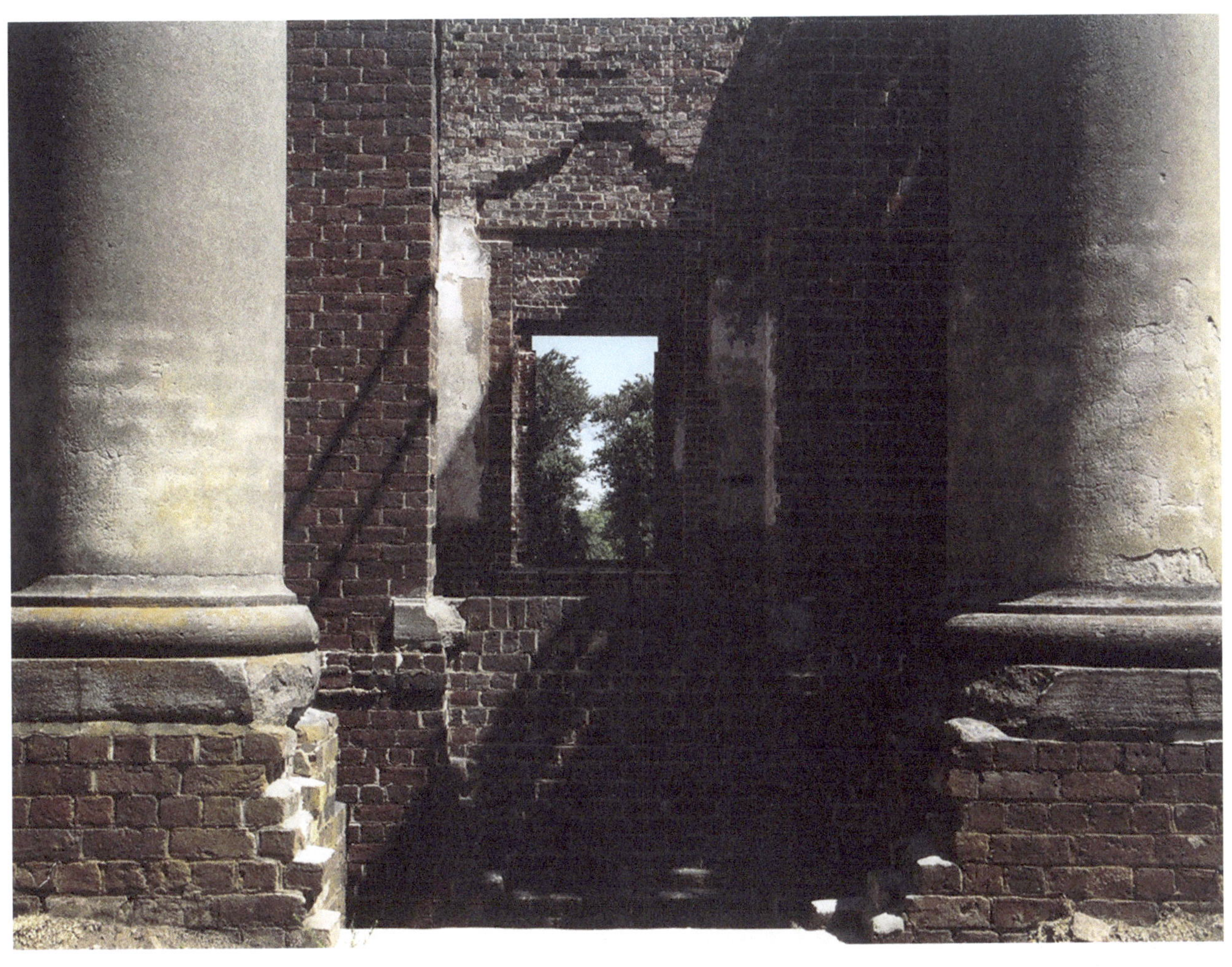

Barboursville, Virginia

A still, small voice.

--Bible, Kings xix. 12

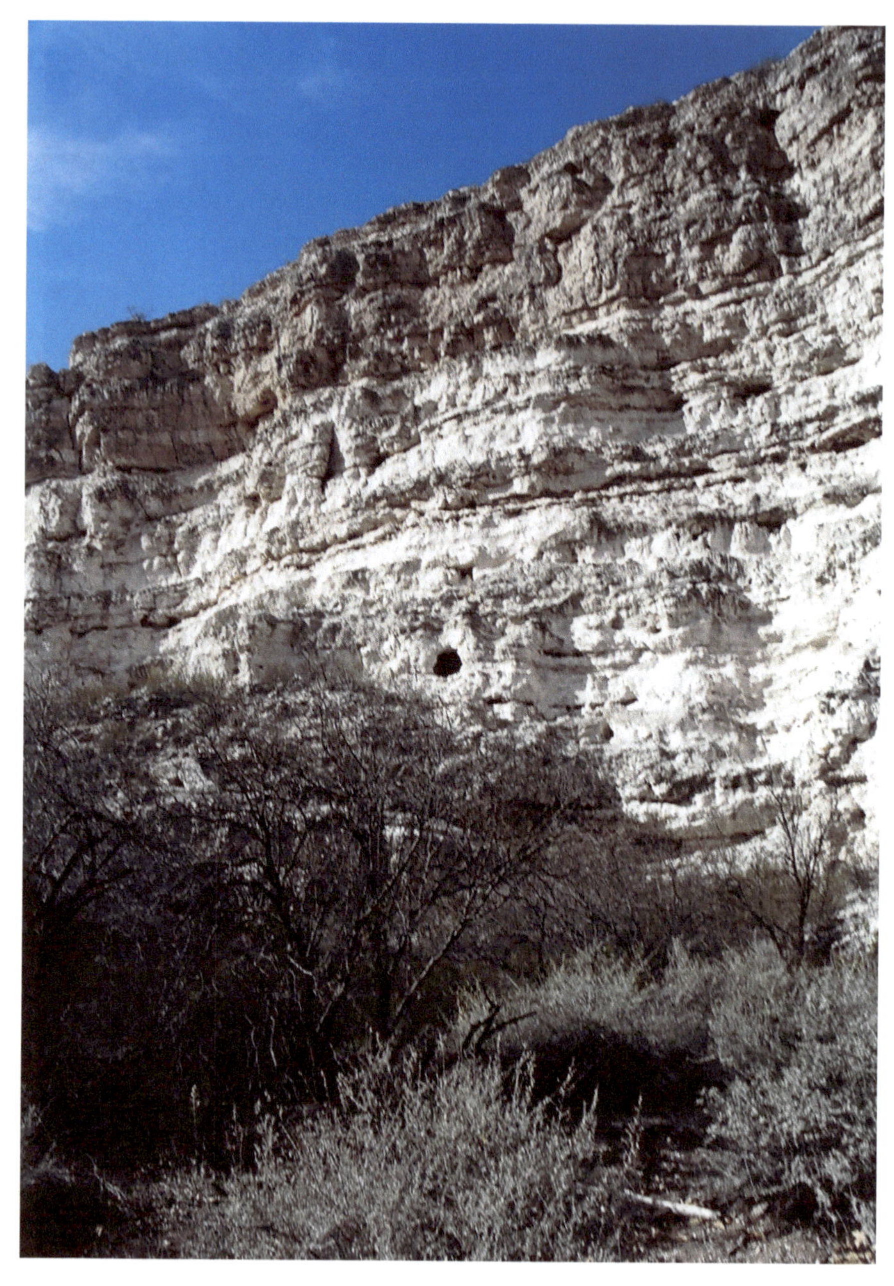

Montezuma Castle National Monument, Arizona

You must trust your intuition--you must trust the small voice inside you which tells you exactly what to say, what to decide.

--Ingrid Bergman, 1915-1982

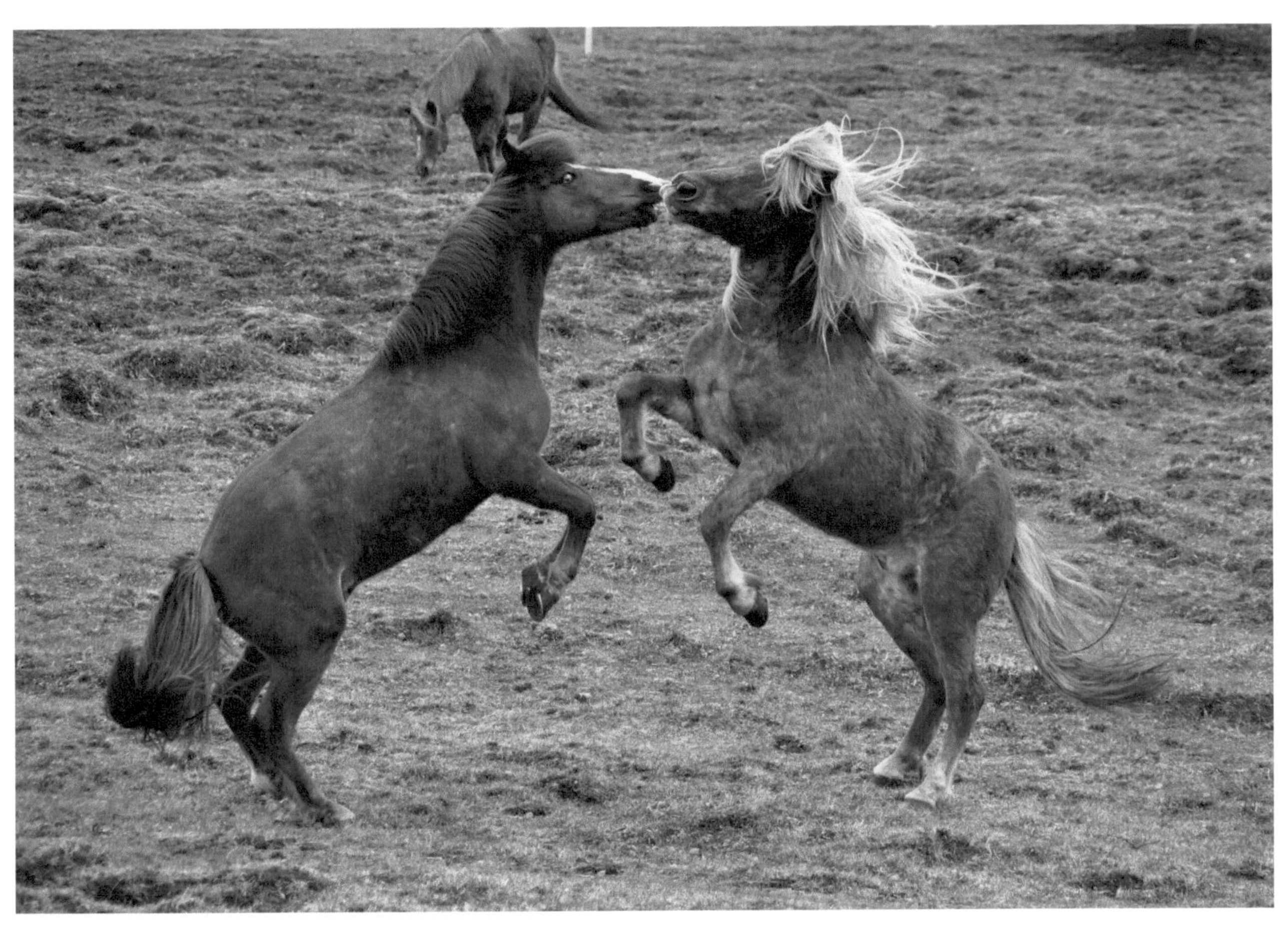

Iceland

One of the saddest lines in the world is,

"Oh come now, be realistic."

The best parts of this world were not fashioned by those who were realistic.

They were fashioned by those who dared to look hard at their wishes

and gave them horses to ride.

--Richard Nelson Bolles, 1927-

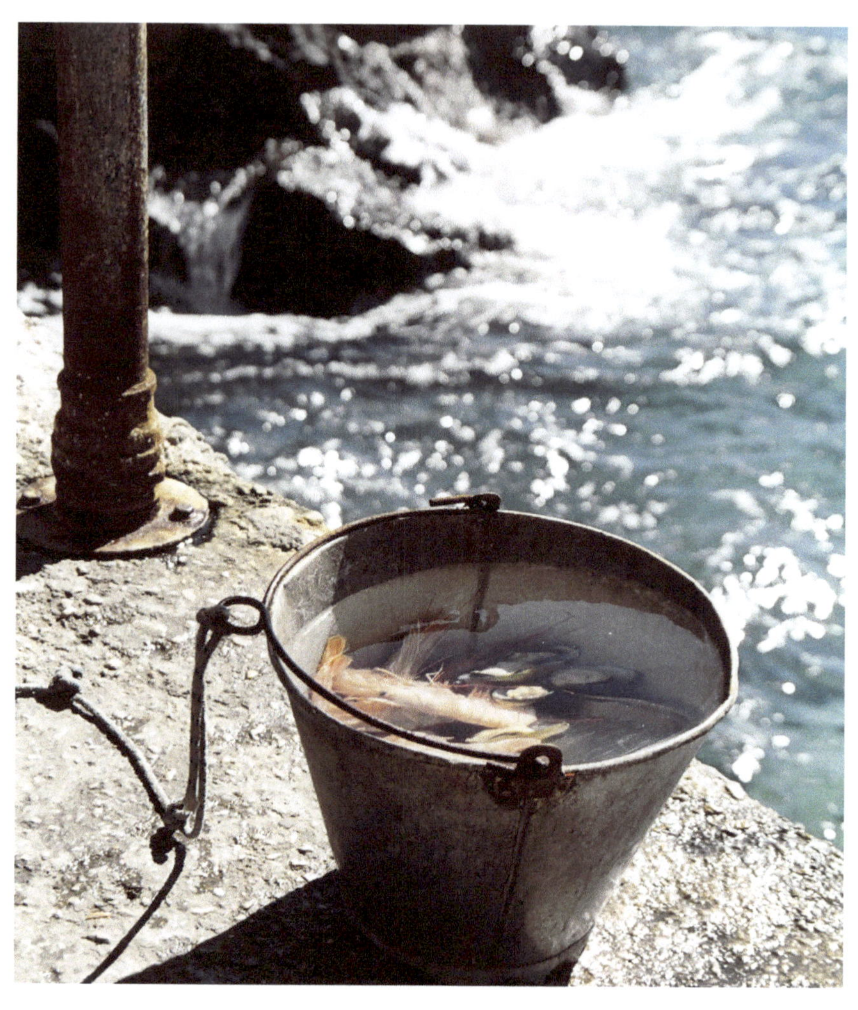

Santorini, Greece

You are the fish you need to catch.

--Anonymous

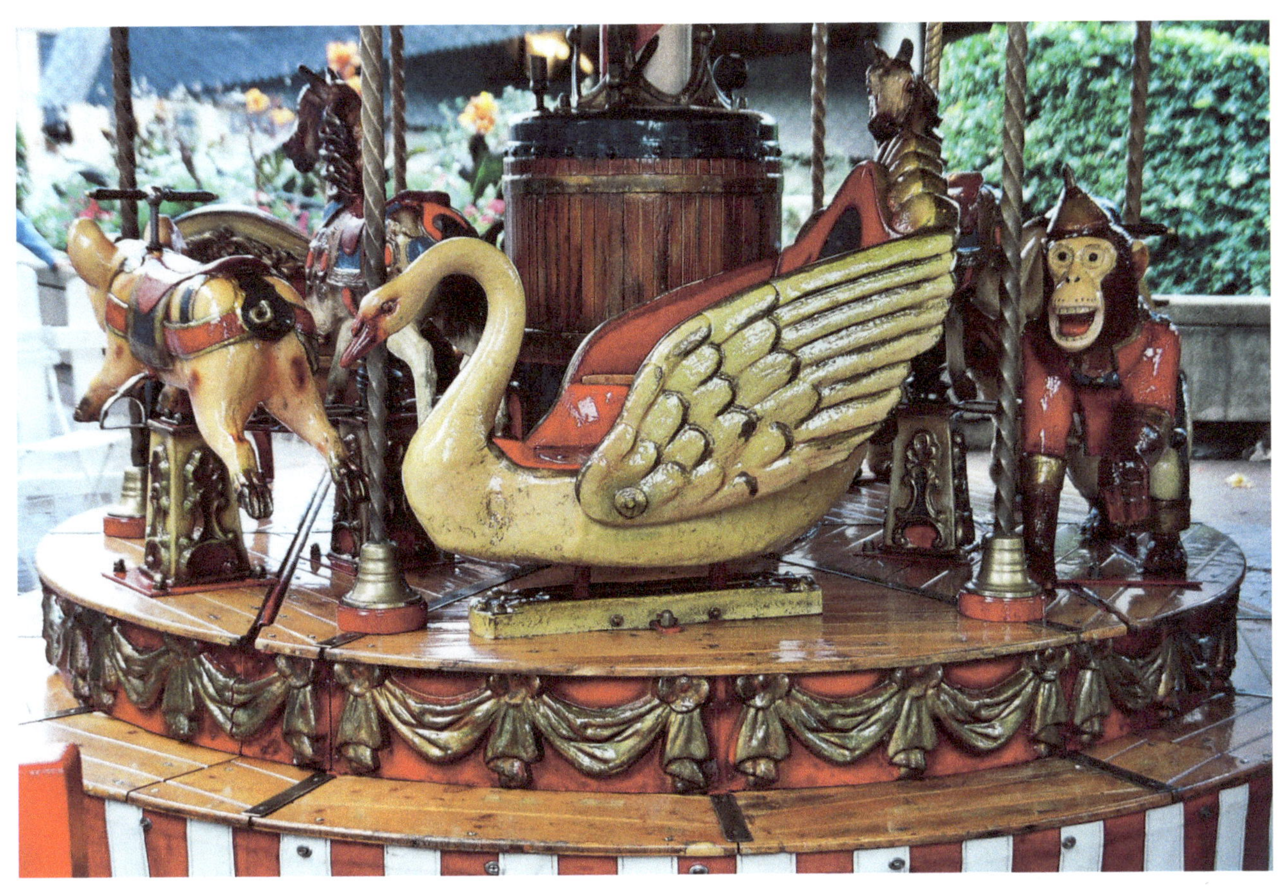

Rouen, France

In every real man a child is hidden that wants to play.

--Friedrich Nietzsche, 1844-1900

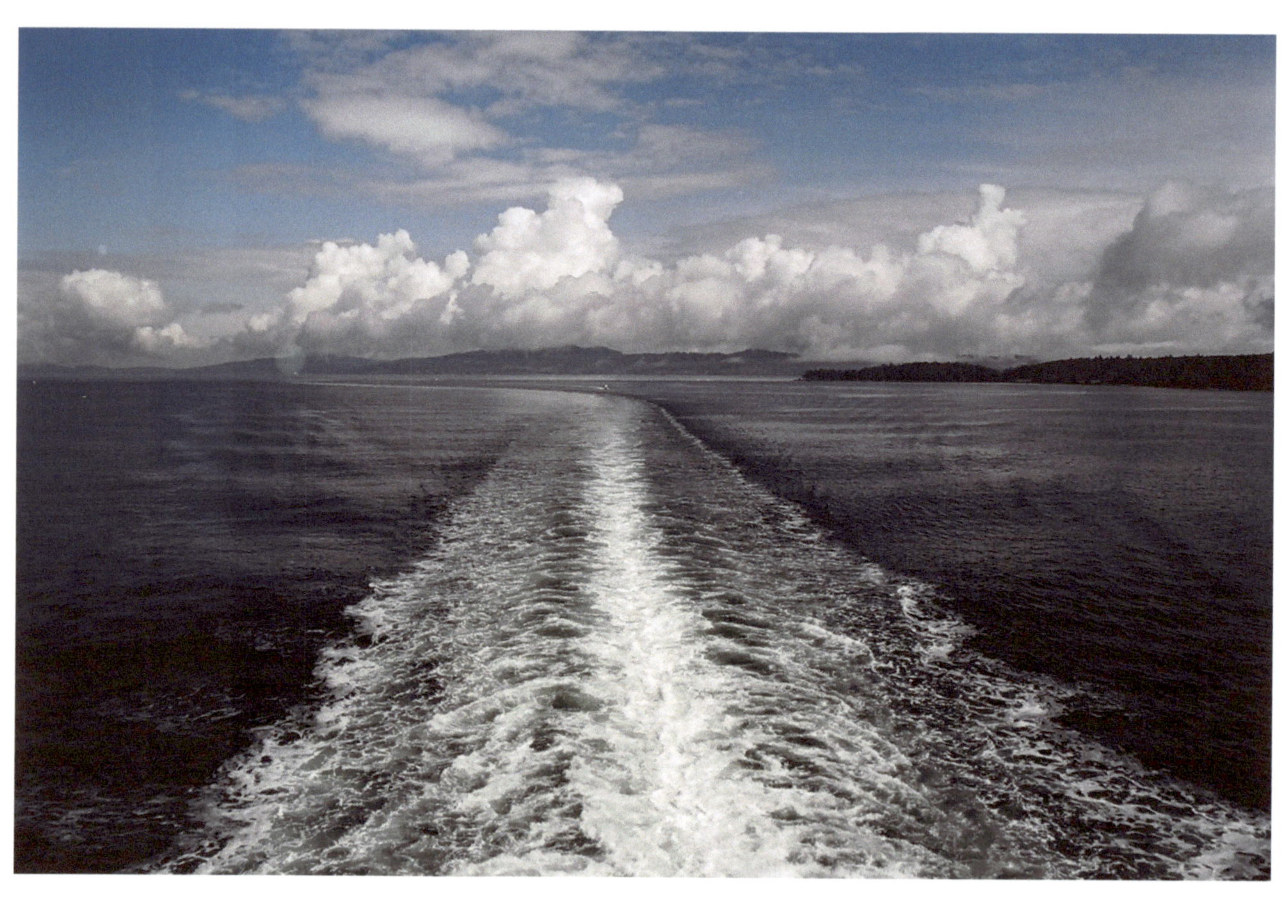

Straight of Georgia, British Columbia

It's as hard to see one's self
as to look backward without turning around.
--Henry David Thoreau, 1817-1862

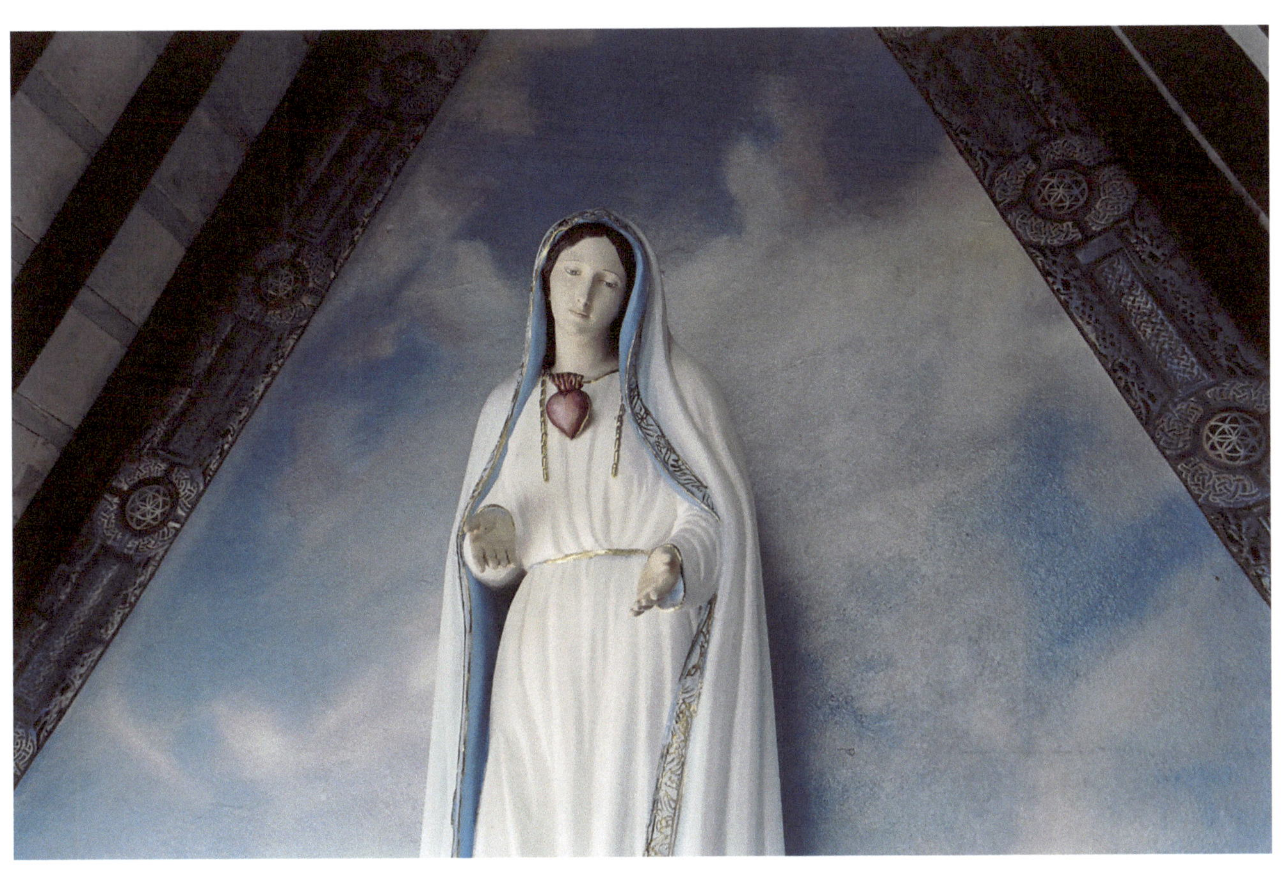

Dingle, Ireland

Each of us makes his own emotional weather, determines the color of the skies in the emotional universe which he inhabits.

--Fulton J. Sheen, 1895-1979

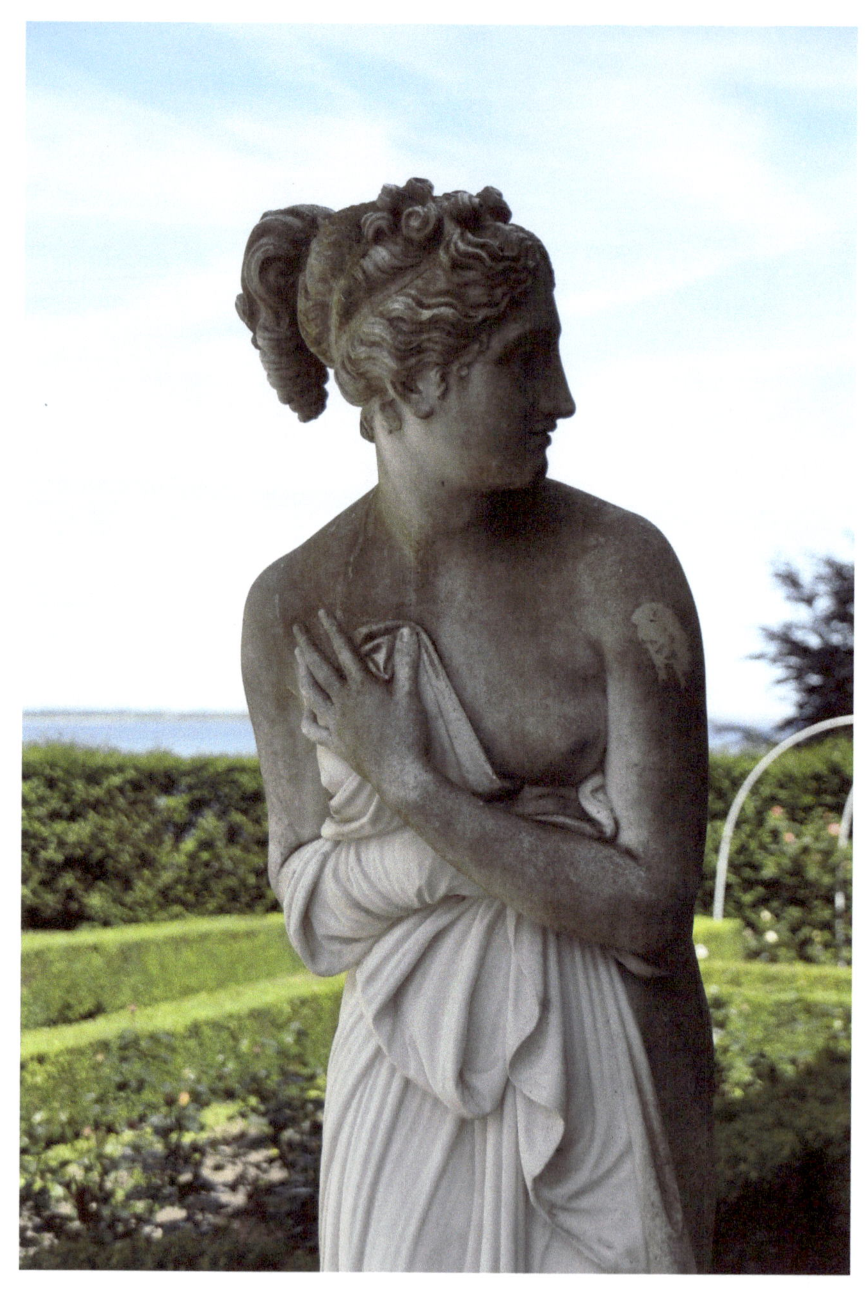

Newport, Rhode Island

When we were children, we used to think that when we were grown-up
we would no longer be vulnerable.
But to grow up is to accept vulnerability...
To be alive is to be vulnerable.
-- Madeleine L'Engle, 1918-2007

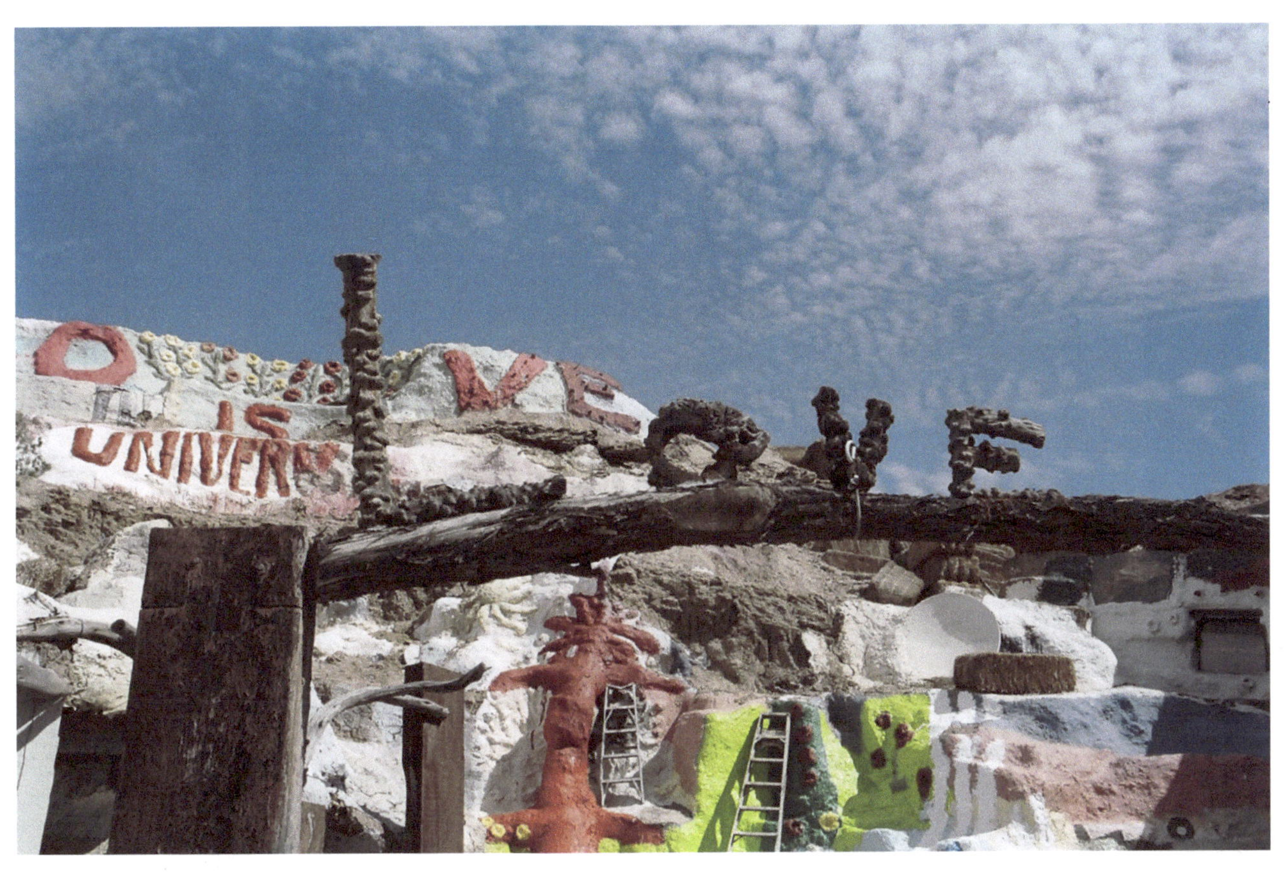

Salvation Mountain, California

For whereas the mind works in possibilities, the intuitions work in actualities, and what you intuitively desire, that is possible to you.

--D.H. Lawrence, 1885-1930

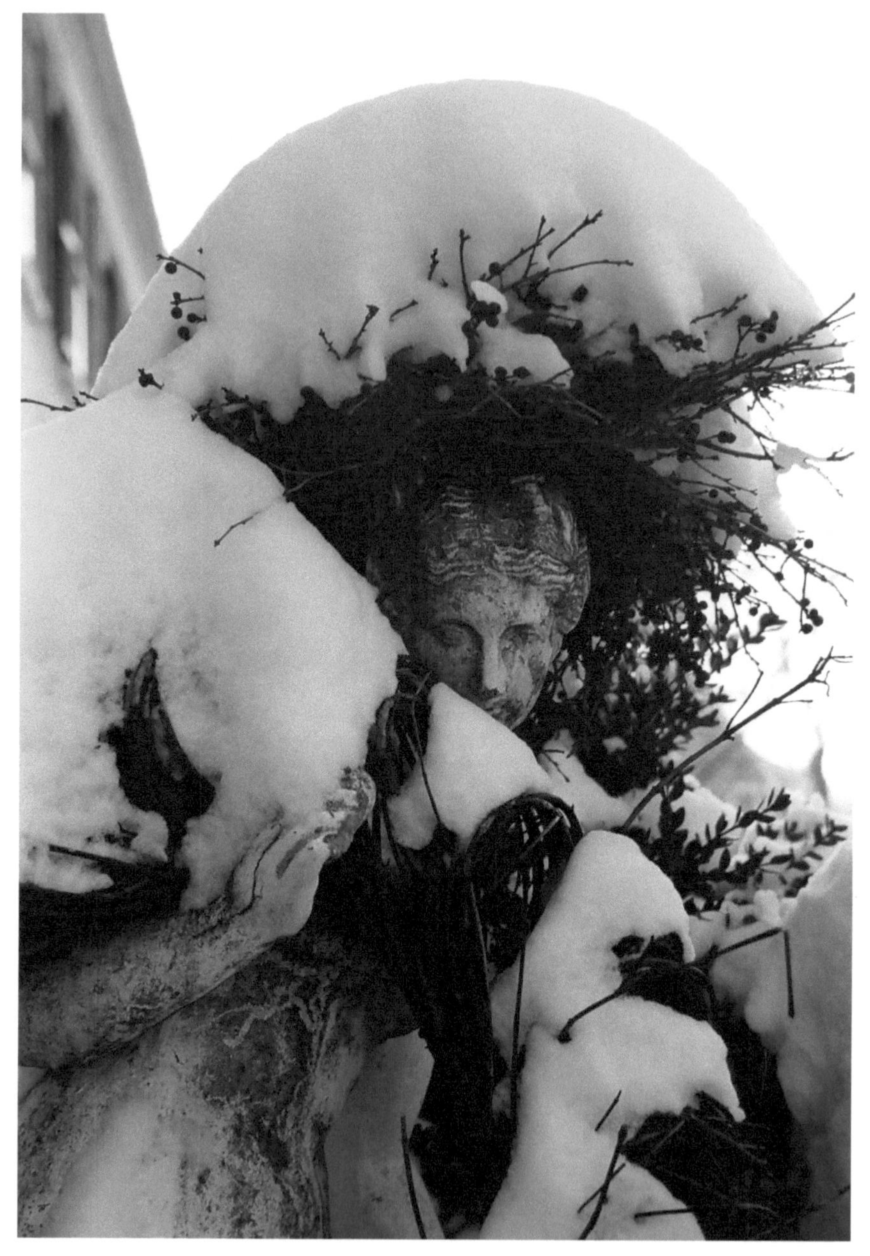

Marblehead, Massachusetts

Life is one long struggle to disinter oneself,
to keep one's head above the accumulations,
the ever deepening layers of objects...
which attempt to cover one over, steadily, almost irresistibly,
like falling snow.
--Rose Macaulay, 1881-1958

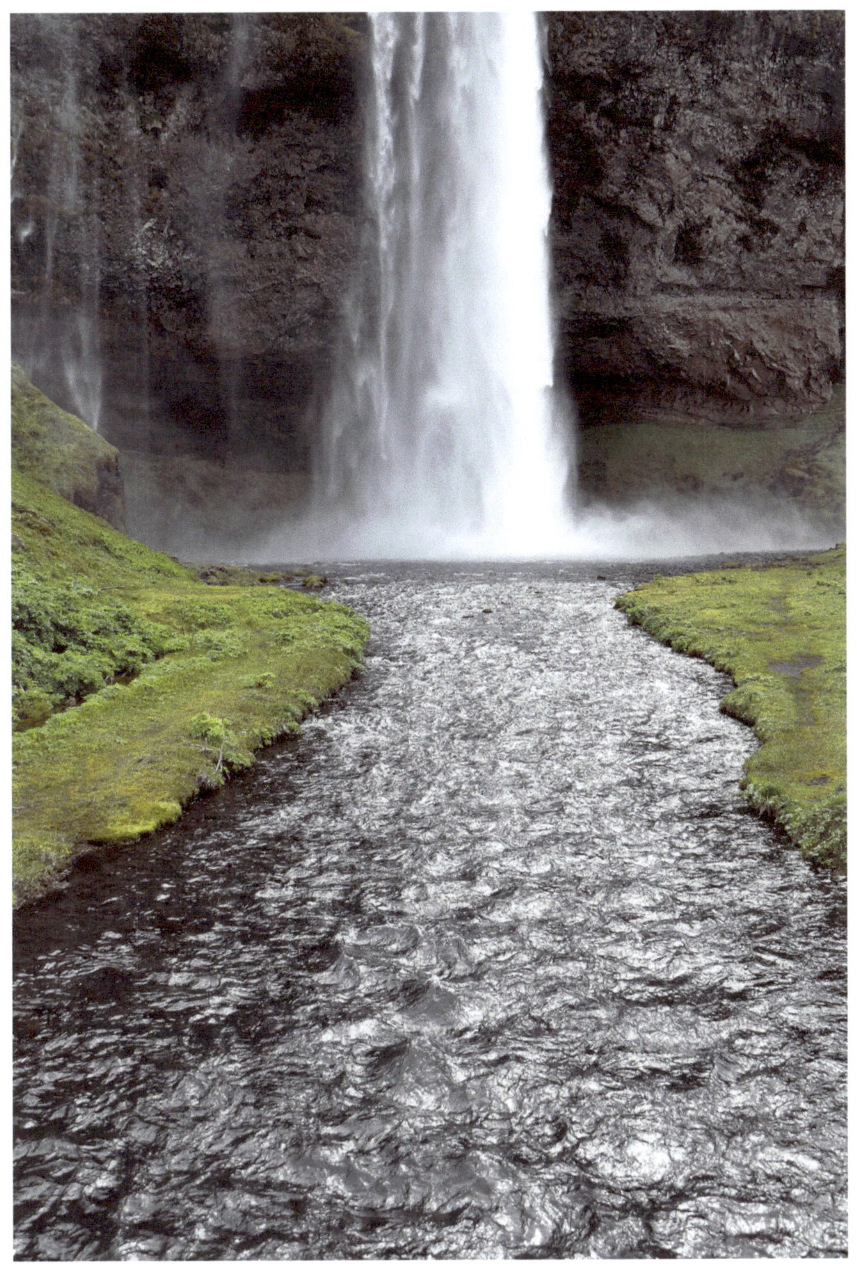

Seljalandsfoss, Iceland

Character--the willingness to accept responsibility for one's own life--
is the source from which self-respect springs.
--Joan Didion, 1934-

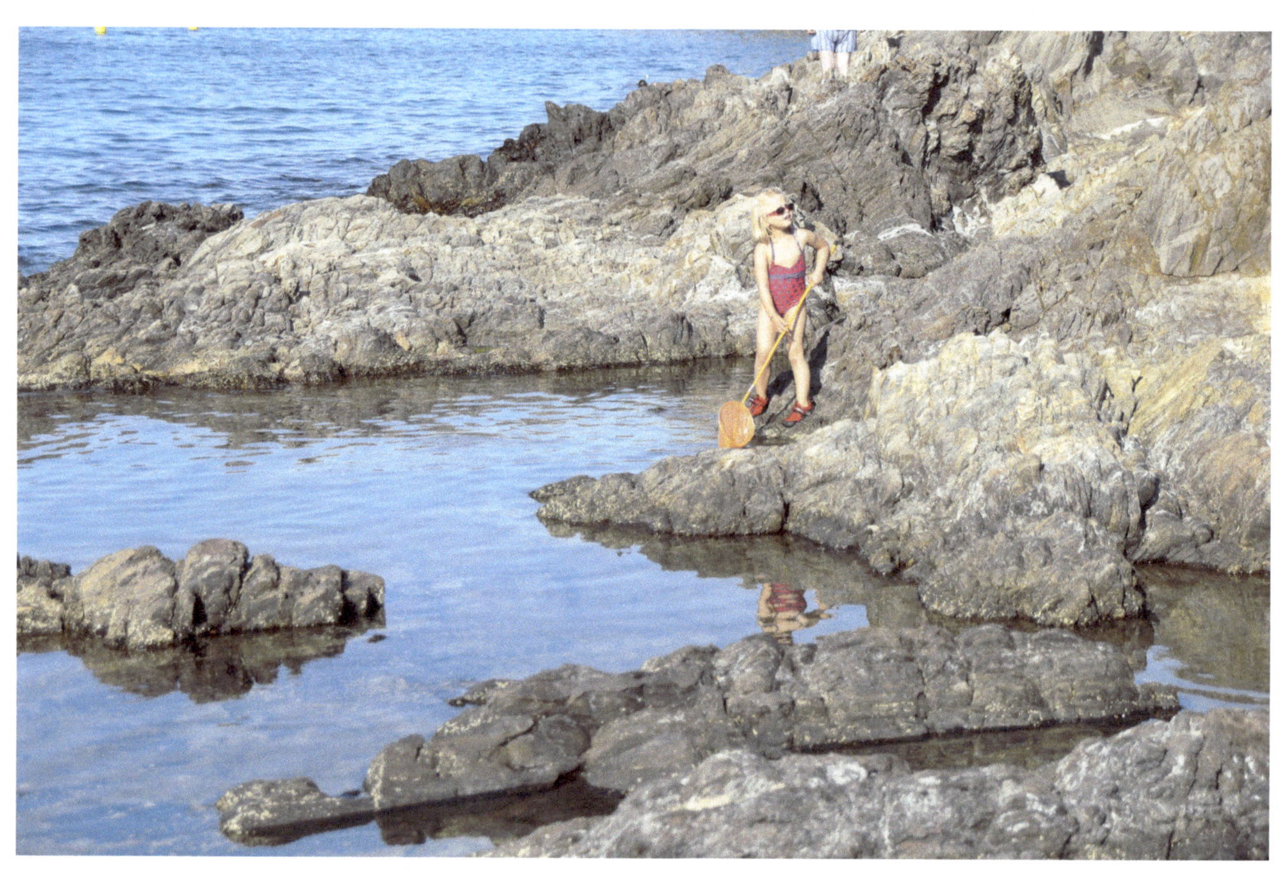

Toulouse, France

Trust yourself. You know more than you think you do.

-Benjamin Spock 1903 -

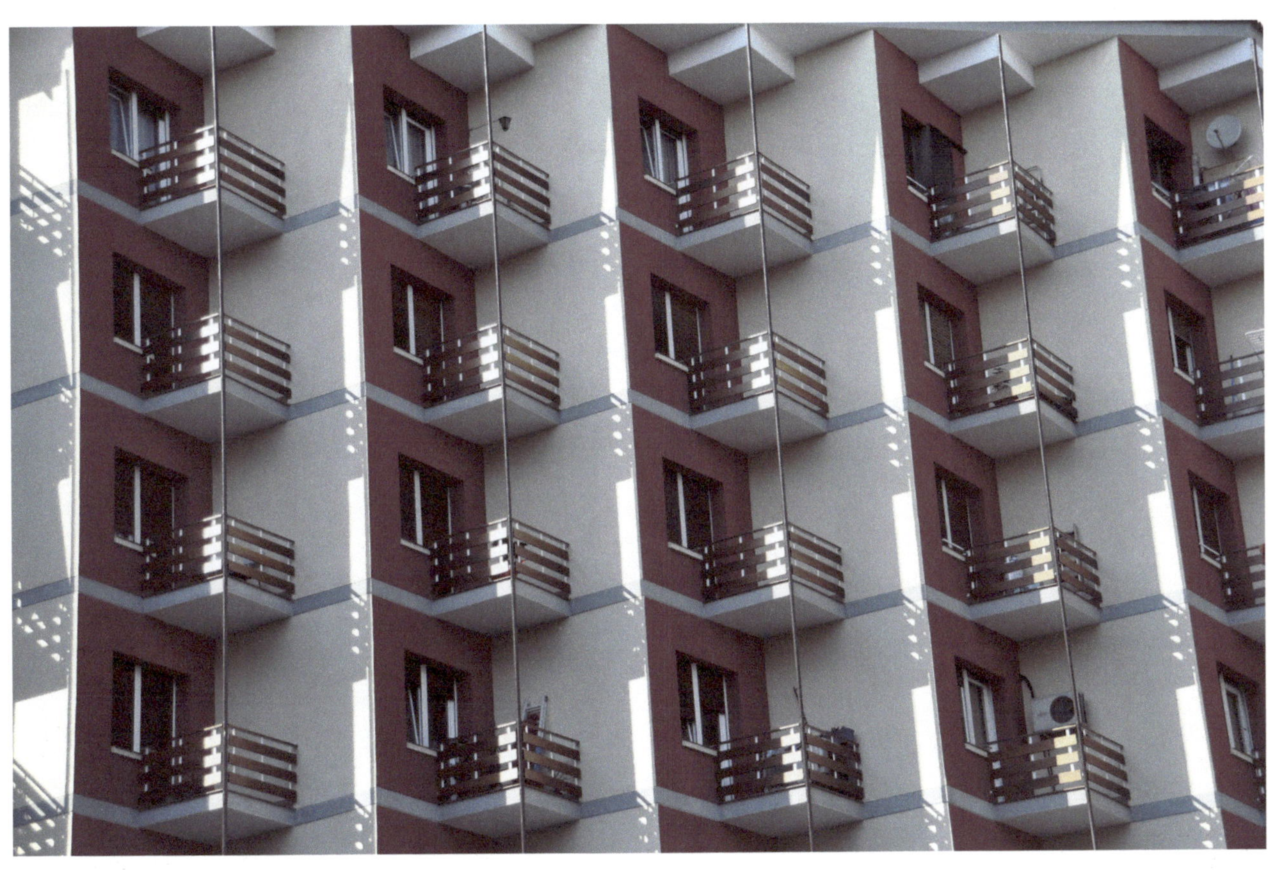

Barcelona, Spain

Dare to be yourself.

– Andre Gide, 1869 – 1951

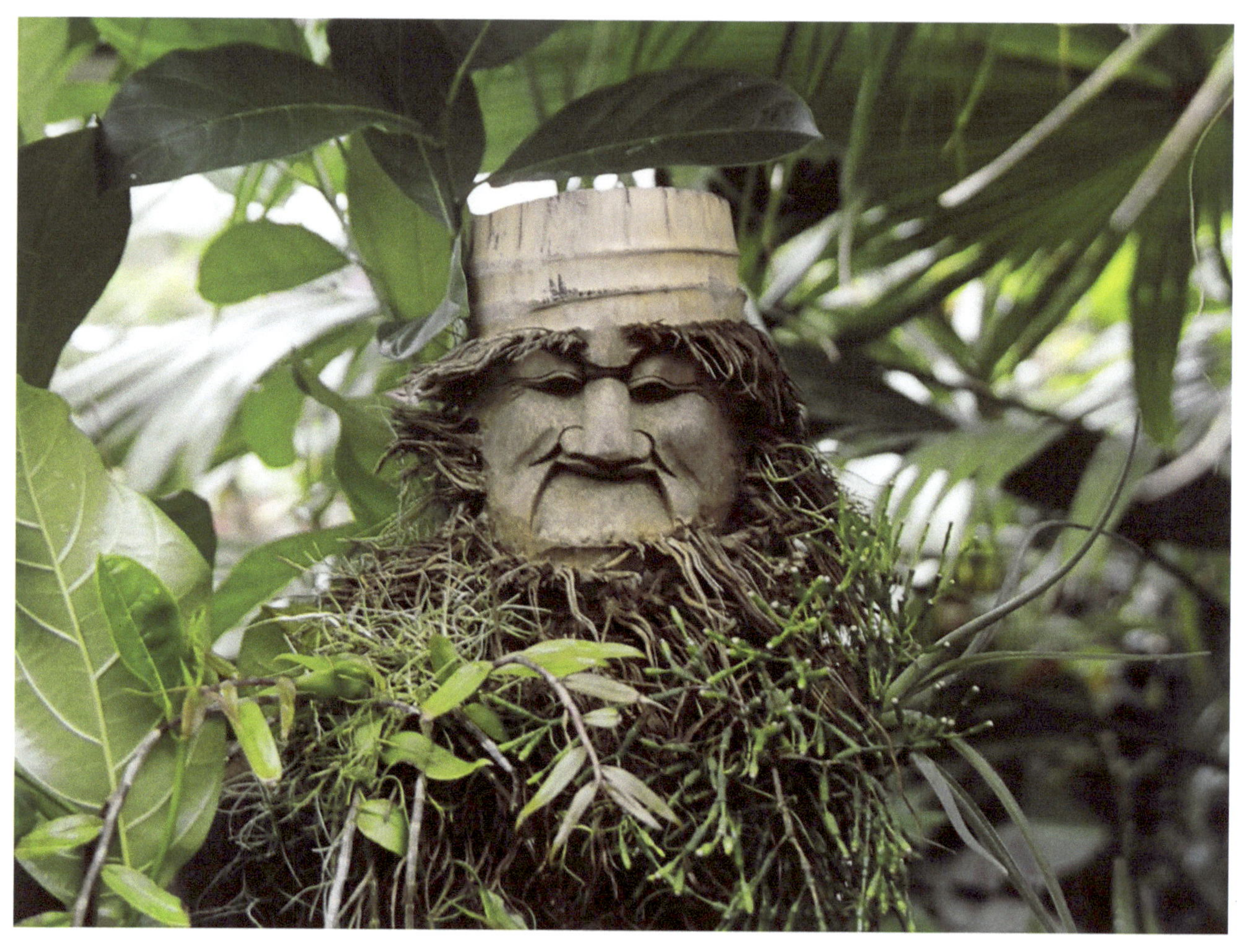

Victoria, British Columbia

Insist on yourself; never imitate.

--Ralph Waldo Emerson, 1803-1882

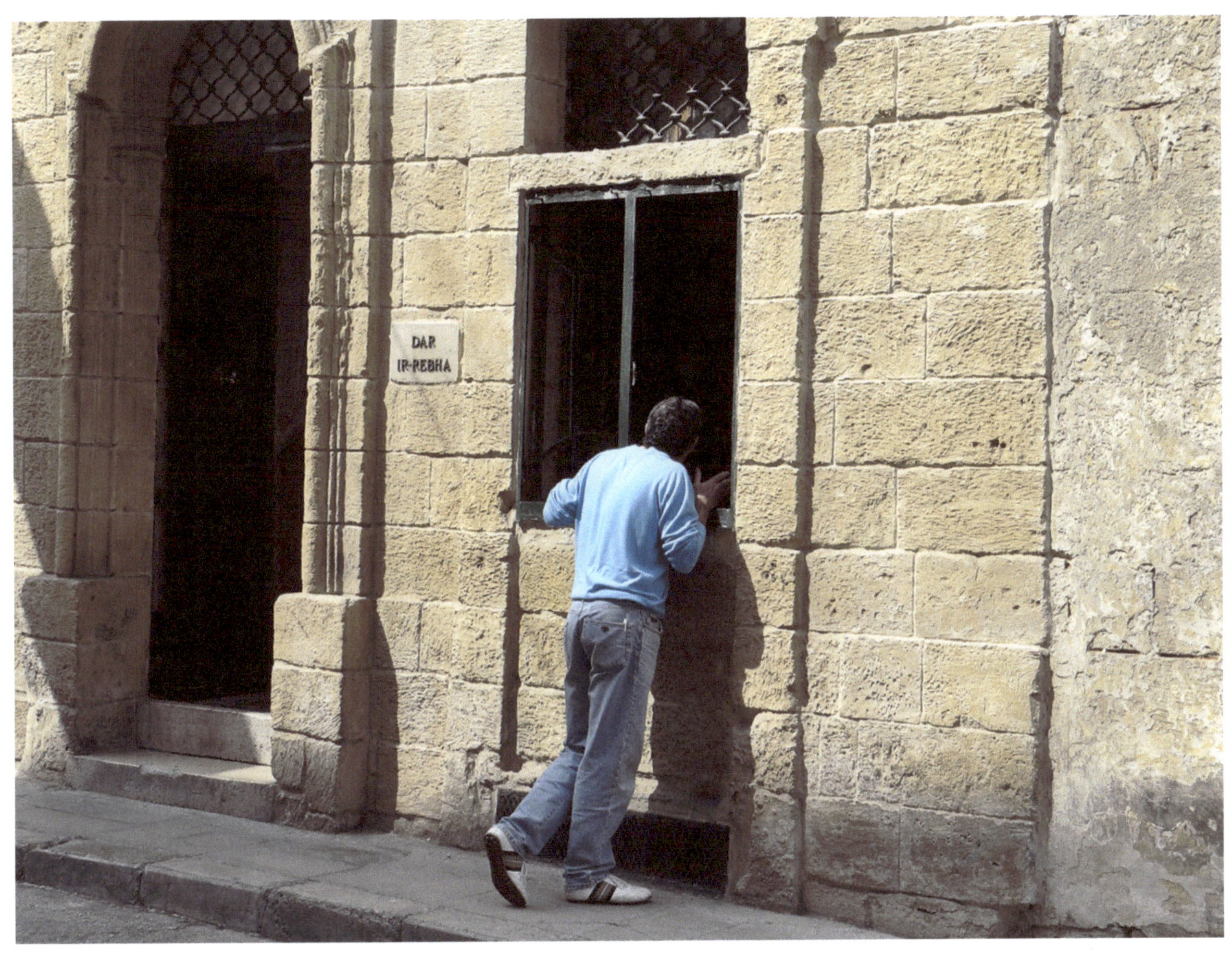

Vittoriosa, Malta

Your vision will become clear only when you can look into your own heart.
Who looks outside, dreams; who looks inside, awakes.
--Carl Gustav Jung, 1875-1961

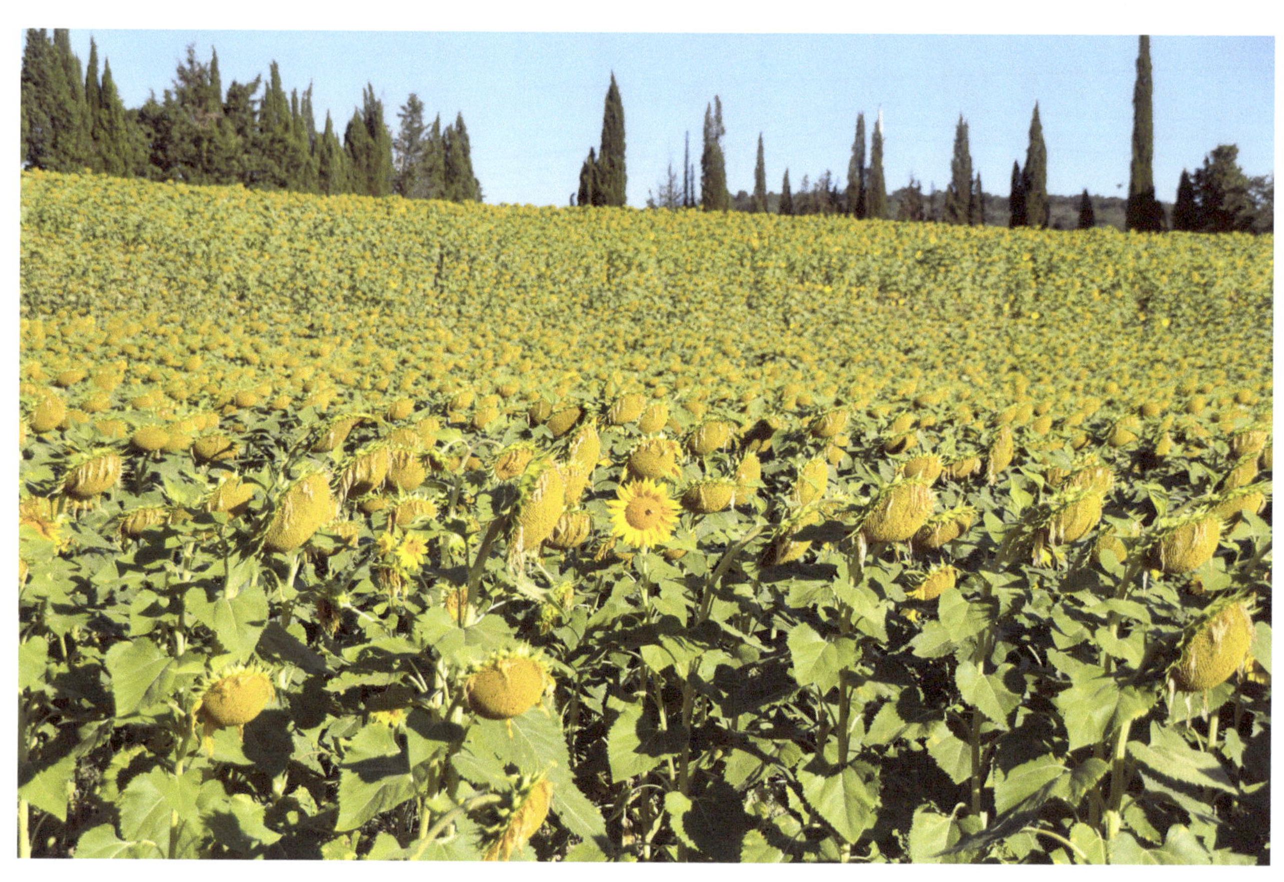

Magrie, France

Get away from the crowd when you can. Keep yourself to yourself,
if only for a few hours daily.
–Arthur Brisbane, 1864 - 1936

Prague, Czech Republic

Teachers open the door. You enter by yourself.

– Chinese Proverb

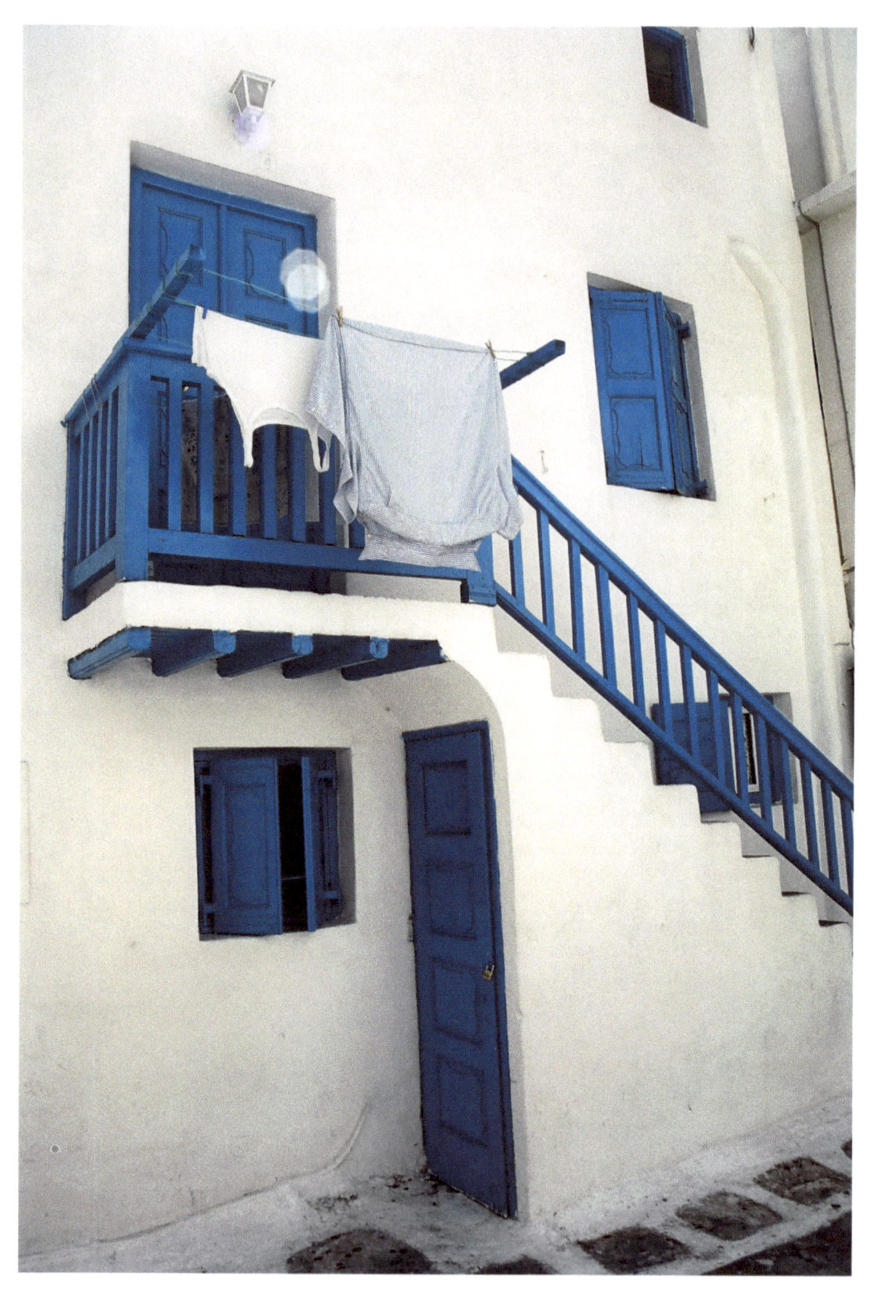

Mykonos, Greece

Happiness cannot be traveled to, owned, earned, worn or consumed.
Happiness is the spiritual experience of living every minute with love, grace and gratitude.
--Denis Waitley, 1924-

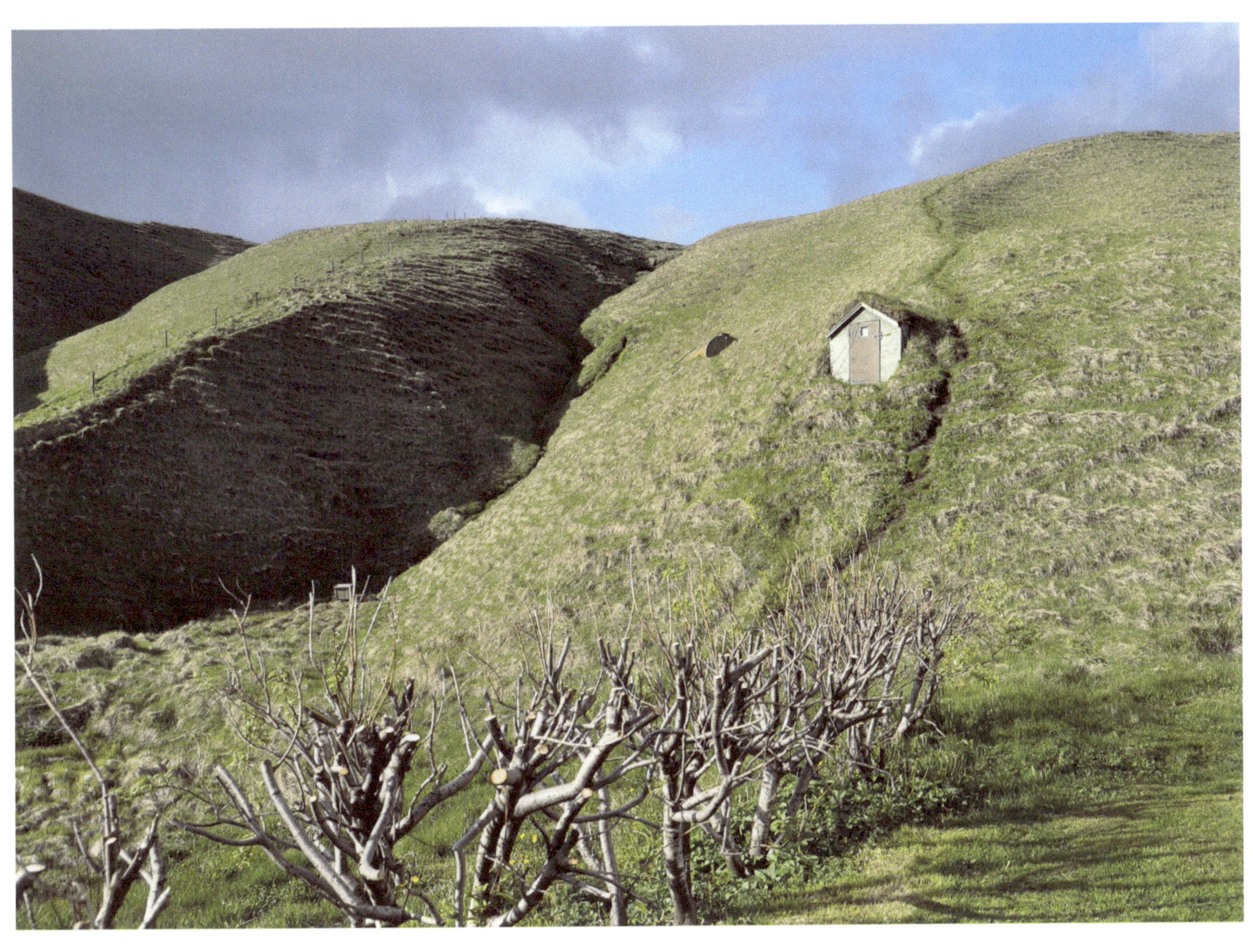

Vik, Iceland

There is only one corner of the universe you can be certain of improving
and that's your own self.
--Aldous Huxley, 1894-1963

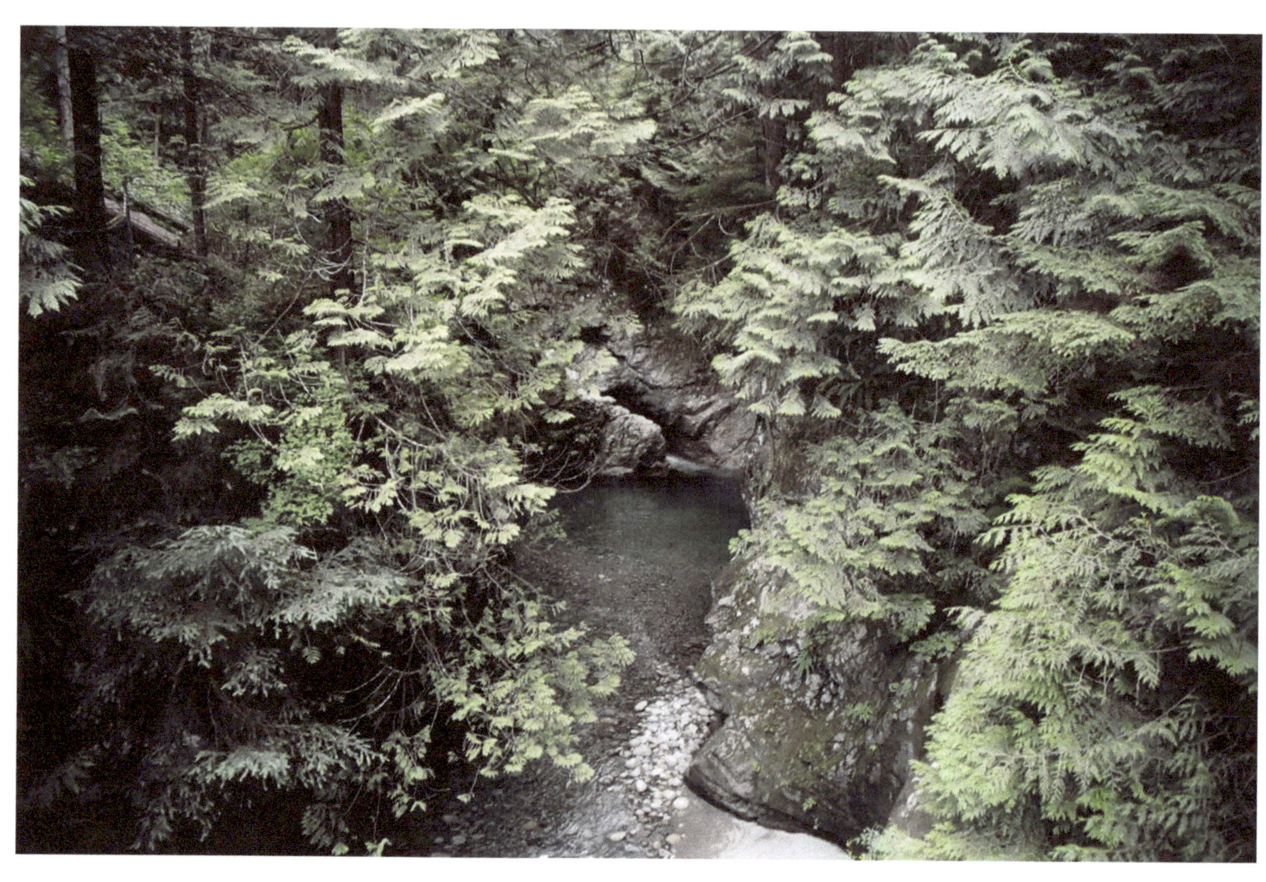

Lynn Canyon, British Columbia

Learn to get in touch with the silence within yourself
and know that everything in this life has a purpose.
--Elisabeth Kubler-Ross, 1926-

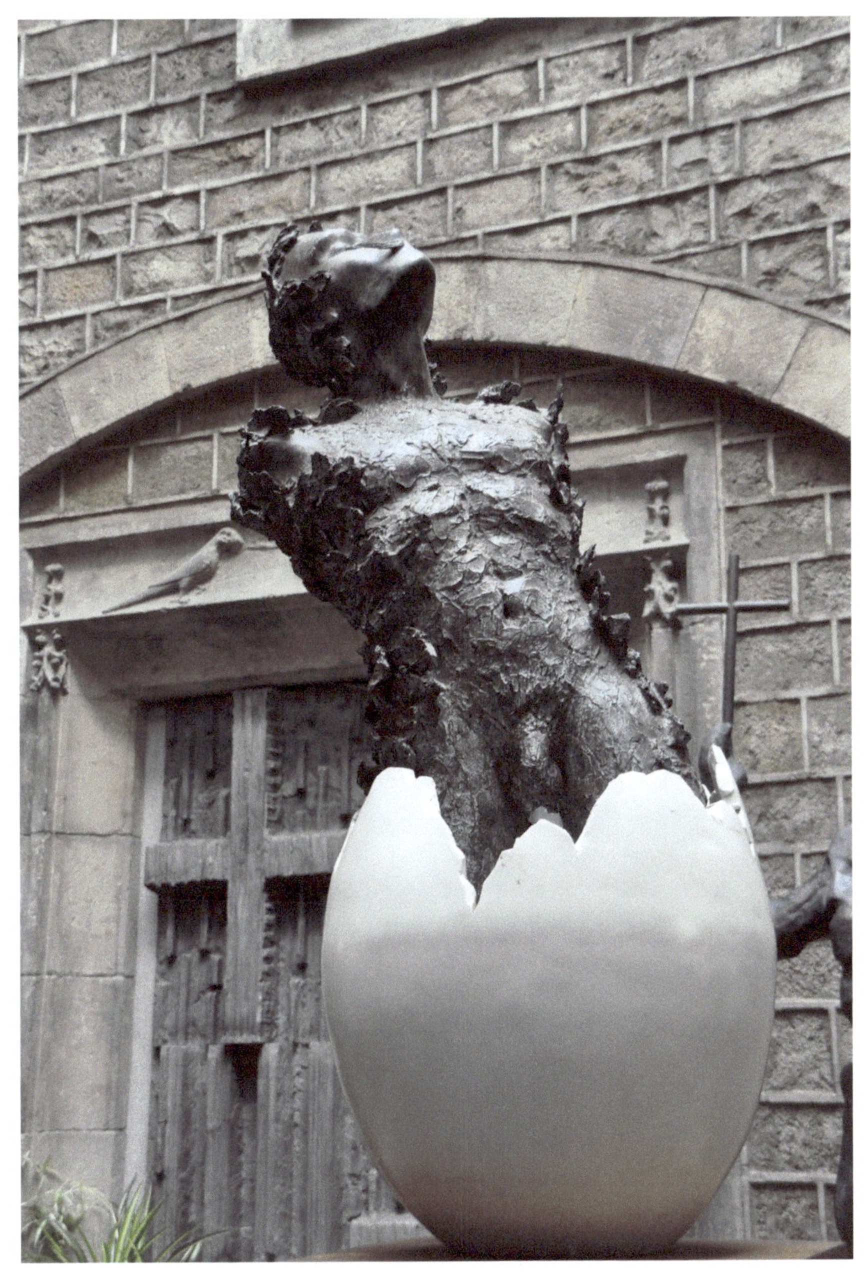

Barcelona, Spain

Living is being born slowly. It would be a little too easy if we could borrow ready-made souls.

– Antoine de Saint Exupery, 1900-1944

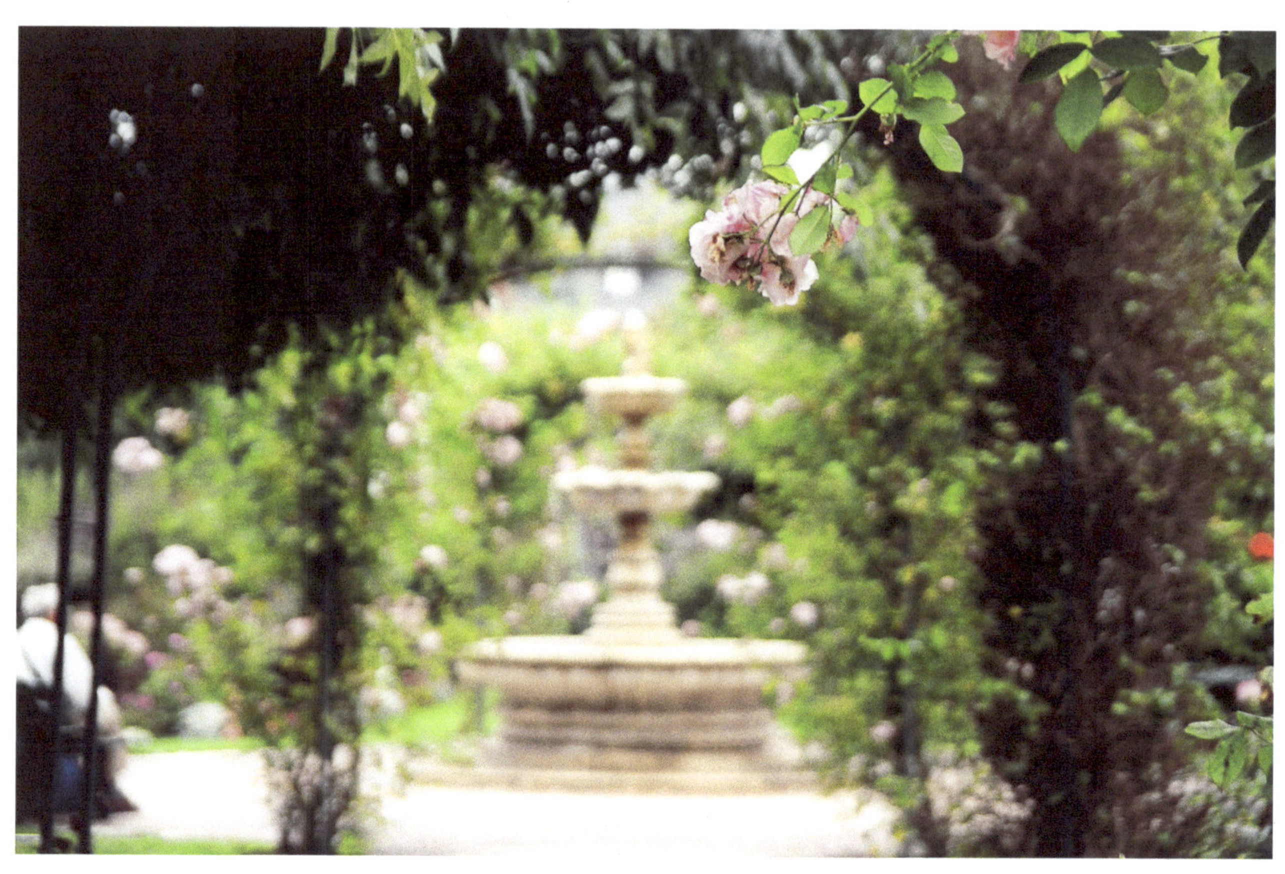

Honfleur, France

A rose is a rose is a rose.

--Gertrude Stein, 1874-1946

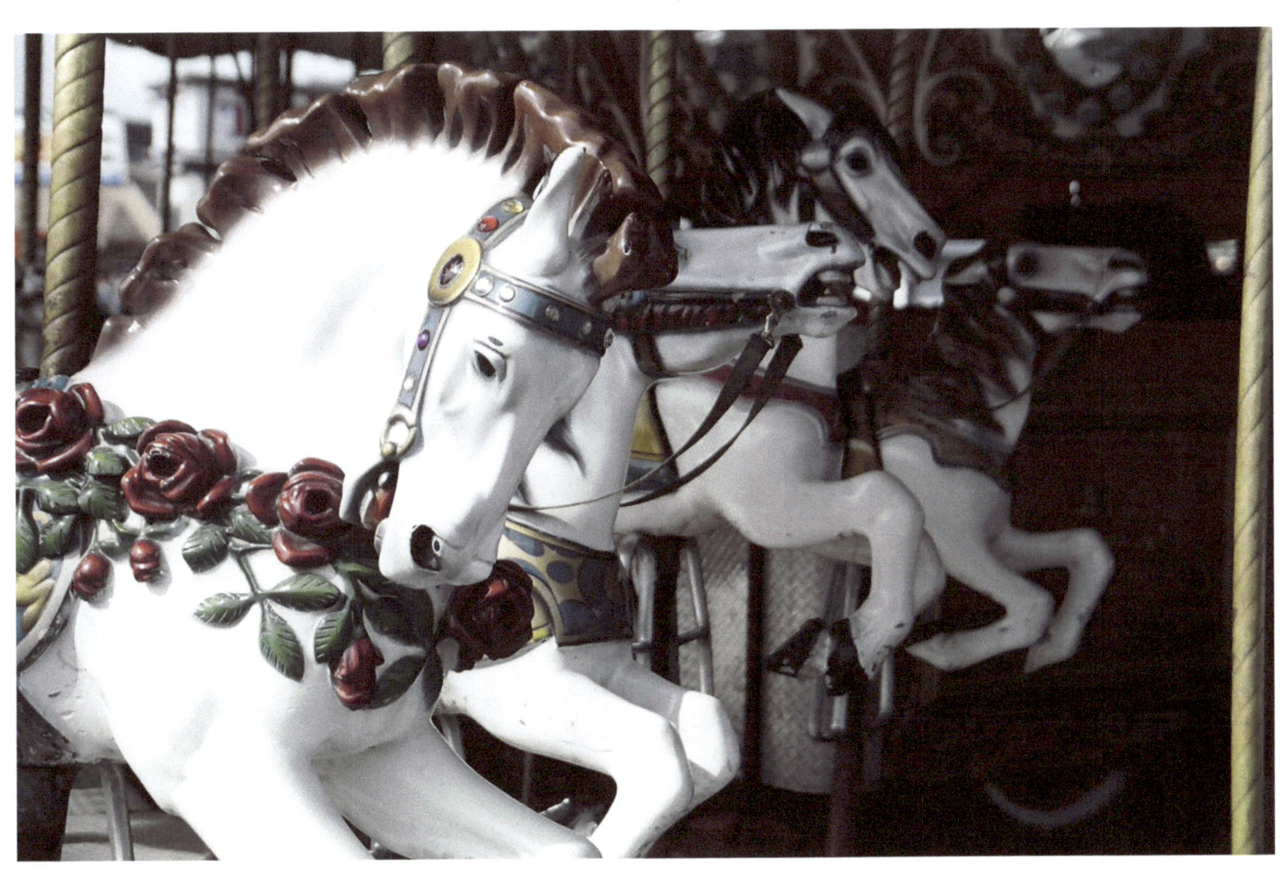

Topsfield, Massachusetts

Never forget that you are one of a kind.
Never forget that if there weren't any need for you
in all your uniqueness to be on earth,
you wouldn't be here in the first place.
--R. Buckminster Fuller, 1893-1983

Bibliography

Dass, Ram, One Liners: A Mini Manual for a Spiritual Life,
Bell Tower, Member of Crown Publishing Group,
a division of Random House, Inc., 2002.

Deger, Steve and Leslie Anne Gibson,
The Little Positive Book of Positive Quotations,
Fairfiew Press, 2006.

Fox, Emmet, Around the Year with Emmet Fox,
Harper San Franciso, a division of HarperCollins Publishers, 1992.

Ratcliffe, Susan, Little Oxford Dictionary of Quotations, New edition,
Oxford University Press, 2005.

Shanahan, John M., The Most Brilliant Thoughts of All Time (in two lines or less),
Collins, an imprint of HarperCollins Publishers, 2005.

Toliver, Wendy, The Little Giant Encyclopedia of Inspirational Quotes,
Sterling Publishing Co., Inc., 2004.

www.bartleby.com
www.famousquotes.com
www.quotationspage.com
www.quotegarden.com
www.quoteland.com
www.quoteworld.org
www.worldofquotes.com
www.viewfromthepier.com

www.ingramcontent.com/pod-product-compliance
Lightning Source LLC
LaVergne TN
LVHW070139110826
845147LV00002B/284

* 9 7 8 0 9 8 2 2 2 0 2 2 1 *